Growing Pains: The Church Hits the Road

STAN CAMPBELL

VICTOR BOOKS®

A DIVISION OF SCRIPTURE PRESS PUBLICATIONS INC.
USA CANADA ENGLAND

BibleLog Series

The Saga Begins
That's the Way the Kingdom Crumbles
Fighters and Writers
What's This World Coming To?
Jesus: God Undercover
Growing Pains: The Church Hits the Road
From the Desk of the Apostle Paul
The Saga Never Ends

BibleLog is an inductive Bible study series for high school students. This eight-book series takes you through the Bible in two years if you study one chapter each week. You may want to use BibleLog in your daily devotions, completing a chapter a week by working through a few pages each day. This book is also designed to be used in group study. A leader's guide with visual aids (reproducible student sheets) is available for each book from your local Christian bookstore or from the publisher.

Second printing, 1989

Scripture taken from the *Holy Bible, New International Version,* © 1973, 1978, 1984, International Bible Society. Used by permission of Zondervan Bible Publishers.

Cover illustration and interior illustrations: John Hawk

Library of Congress Catalog Card Number: 88-62859
ISBN: 0-89693-384-9

Recommended Dewey Decimal Classification: 248.83
Suggested Subject Heading: YOUTH—RELIGIOUS LIFE

CONTENTS

INTRODUCTION

Welcome to Book 6 of the BibleLog Series, *Growing Pains: The Church Hits the Road*. As you go through this book, you'll discover the reason for the title. When Jesus was on Earth, He was the One that drew most of the criticism from those opposed to what He was saying. But after He returned to His Father in heaven, His followers began to encounter persecution. And as the church experienced growth, it also experienced growing pains in the form of opposition and hostility from others—even to the point where church members had to die for what they believed.

The Book of Acts is a historical account of God's involvement in the establishment of His church and contains many fascinating stories of His power and love. You'll meet a number of new people in Acts that you may not have known or perhaps have forgotten about. Later, in Romans and 1 Corinthians, the personal element takes precedent over the historical. You'll get to read someone else's mail, so to speak. And you'll see that the very first churches ever formed probably had a number of the same good and bad points that your own church has today.

Commit to do one session each week. You need a Bible (the author uses the NIV) and this book. It won't take all that long to complete a session, and you will be able to go through the Old Testament in one year and the New Testament in one year.

At the end of each session you will find a section called Journey Inward. This section will challenge you to apply a portion of what you have just studied to your daily life. It's your opportunity to go a little further each week in your relationship with God.

May your journey through Acts, Romans, and 1 Corinthians be one filled with new insights, bold challenges, and helpful promises!

TONGUES OF FIRE, TONGUES OF LIARS

(Acts 1—5)

It was time for the class reunion at Main Street High. A mere 10 years ago, the school "paroled" a couple of hundred insecure, immature graduates. Many went on to college. Others went to vocational schools. Some went right to work. And tonight most of them were going to reassemble in the gymnasium to "mingle" (according to the invitation), but more truthfully to check each other out to see who had become a success and who hadn't.

David was looking forward to this night. In high school he had been "Mr. Average"—average grades, average looks, not quite good enough to be completely accepted by the "cool" people, but not a total reject either. Since high school, David had worked hard to become a top psychologist. He had also grown a beard, gotten in shape by working out at a health club, and improved his wardrobe considerably. He was correct in assuming that no one would recognize him for a while, and he used his anonymity to observe everyone else.

He first staked out Charlotte. She had been the gossip columnist for the school paper, so it hadn't taken long for her to volunteer to organize the reunion. She was still eager to scoop all the tidbits she could, and her post at the doorway gave her immediate access to everyone's personal history—who was married, divorced, pregnant, fat, bald, and so forth. Charlotte spent the whole night watching for expensive cars to pull up and then fawning over their owners to try to regain their friendship (or some facsimile of friendship). David could tell that Charlotte was still tolerated by others, but not genuinely liked.

While David was watching Charlotte scout out the fancy cars, he was surprised to see one particular person get out of a new Mercedes—Jimmy Gekko (or "Jimmy the Geek," as he used to be called). Jimmy had been a quiet, somewhat misunderstood person in high school. While the other guys had focused their attention on girls and cars, Jimmy was hacking away at his computer keyboard. Jim had been the source of many jokes back then, but had since become the president of a successful, growing computer software company.

Another surprise was Jimmy's wife, Lola. All David could remember about Lola from high school was how stuck-up she had been. He was shocked that she and Jimmy had ever gotten together. But it turned out that they made a very nice couple. Lola explained that she had done a lot of "growing up" during college when she met a number of other snobby girls (like herself). She saw what lousy friends they were. And when Lola saw many of her own bad points reflected in others, she decided to change her attitude and make as many genuine friends as she could. One of those new friends was Jimmy, and as they say, "the rest was history."

David, Jim, and Lola decided to hang around together, and they saw a lot of eye-opening things that night. It turned out that many of the cheerleaders and sports jocks who had been so popular in high school hadn't been able to cut it in real life. Many of the people who had cheated their way through high school hadn't been able to get through college. A lot of them had been forced to take jobs that didn't come close to letting them maintain the lifestyle they would have liked. The smart ones, like Lola, had wised up and worked hard to improve themselves. But others continued to lead shallow lives, refusing to admit that anything had changed since high school. When those people got together, they still acted like they were the only important people on earth. They seemed to think that they were still too good to associate closely with most of the other people at the reunion.

By this time, David was taking notes for a future article in *Psychology Today*. The psychologist in him noticed that the happiest people seemed to be the ones who had developed a high degree of . . . what word was he looking for? . . . perhaps integrity. Yes, that was the right word. People with integrity had learned to like themselves for who they were. They refused to put on an act just to impress others. They were honest with themselves and their friends. They didn't enter relationships only to see how they could personally benefit from them. They were people that others liked to be around.

As David outlined his article in his head, he smiled as he realized that it was going to be a good one. And after all he had learned at this reunion, he lived (for the most part) happily ever after.

JOURNEY ONWARD

If you recently completed Book 5 of this series, *Jesus: God Undercover,* then you know that Jesus had encouraged and modeled a life of humility. He wanted His followers to be satisfied with whatever they had. And He challenged them to lead lives of integrity, so that no one could question their motives or beliefs.

But Jesus had ascended into heaven. His followers were concerned about what lay ahead in their futures. And it is at this crucial point in their lives that the Book of Acts begins. (Acts was written by Luke, and it picks up at just about the same point where the Gospel of Luke left off. Both books are addressed to a friend of Luke's named Theophilus.

Keep in mind that Luke was a doctor, so look closely for his ability to notice details as you read through this book.) The issue of integrity continues throughout this session. As you work your way through, try to mentally list the areas of your life in which integrity plays a major role.

Where were Jesus' followers to go after His return to heaven? (Acts 1:1-5)

What had been Jesus' plan for His disciples? (1:6-8)

What did the disciples do while they waited for further instructions? (1:9-14)

There were about 120 believers at this time. It doesn't seem like a lot of people, considering Jesus had conducted a public ministry for about three years. But as you will see, Jesus knew what He was doing. What was one of the first items of business that this group of 120 people took care of? (1:15-26)

PENTECOST
The Jews had a celebration called the Feast of Weeks, which came fifty days after the Sabbath of Passover Week (Leviticus 23:15-16). This feast was also called Pentecost. Since Jesus had been crucified at Passover (John 19:31) and had remained on Earth another forty days (Acts 1:3), this particular Pentecost was just about ten days after Jesus had

returned to heaven. And on this specific day of Pentecost, some unusual events took place. Describe the things that happened (Acts 2:1-4).

How did the followers of Jesus get the attention of the visitors to Jerusalem? (2:5-12)

Many people were amazed by the newly acquired ability of Jesus' followers, but not everyone. How did some people try to explain it away? (2:13)

How did Peter explain it? (2:14-21)

Peter went on to deliver a short sermon. He reminded the people of the miracles that Jesus had performed (2:22), of His willing death (2:23), and of His resurrection (2:24-36). Peter's speech left his listeners a little confused. How did they respond? (2:37)

Then they wanted to know what they should do. What did Peter tell them? (2:38-40)

After seeing the effects of the power of the Holy Spirit, did many people accept Peter's offer? (2:41)

How did all these people relate to each other? Be specific and describe the kind of attitudes the early believers had toward one another (2:42-47).

MORE MIRACLES

It is evident from the events that took place on the day of Pentecost that God was able to do miraculous things even when Jesus was not physically present in human form. The Jewish religious leaders had assumed that the followers of Jesus were just a cult that would fizzle out after their leader was taken from them. But they were soon to discover that God's power could be displayed in any number of ways. Describe one situation that provided an opportunity for Peter and John to show someone what God could do for him (3:1-5).

How did Peter and John use this opportunity to demonstrate God's power as Jesus might have? (3:6-8)

How did this miracle affect the people who saw or heard about it? (3:9-10)

Again, Peter responded to their confusion with a sermonette (which was probably not too easy with a guy hanging on to him [3:11]). How did Peter explain the miracle that had taken place? (3:11-13)

Then Peter reminded the Jewish people of their recent actions toward
Jesus, and he didn't beat around the bush. He pointed out that:
(1) Even though Pilate wanted to let Jesus go, the Jews had insisted
that He be killed; (2) They had demanded that a murderer (Barabbas)
be released instead of God's holy Son; and (3) Even though they had
killed Jesus, God had raised Him from the dead.

Peter realized that the people had acted in ignorance. He reminded
them that Scripture had foretold Christ's suffering at the hands of His
own people. What did Peter suggest that the people do? (3:17-21)

What reasons did Peter give to persuade the people to act on his suggestion? (3:22-26)

When the religious authorities got wind of what Peter and John were
saying, how did they respond? (4:1-2)

What happened to Peter and John? (4:3)

What happened to the people who had heard Peter and John? (4:4)

The next day Peter and John were called before the religious leaders to
explain themselves. These were the same leaders who had been in
charge of the proceedings to have Jesus killed. And it should come as

no surprise by now that Peter responded to their questions with another minisermon. He again focused on the Jewish leaders' role in having Jesus killed, God's power in having Him raised from the dead, and scriptural prophecies that applied to the situation (4:5-12).

The religious leaders didn't know what to say in response to Peter's words. Why not? (4:13-14)

The religious leaders called a meeting to decide what to do with Peter and John. What did they finally decide? (4:15-18)

How did Peter and John respond to that decision? (4:19-20)

How did the defiance of Peter and John affect the decision of the Sanhedrin? Why? (4:21-22)

How did the followers of Jesus respond when Peter and John were released? (4:23-30)

What motivation did they all have to continue proclaiming the Gospel? (4:31)

In their personal lives, how did the believers demonstrate that total obedience to Jesus was an effective way to live? (4:32-35)

What person is introduced at this time, and what was his nickname? (4:36-37—Remember this guy because he will pop up again later.)

SERIOUS CONSEQUENCES

With such a giving spirit among the followers of Jesus, it was bound to happen that someone would come along and ruin it. Who took an improper attitude toward giving, and what did they do? (5:1-2)

Why do you think these people did what they did?

Do you think that what they did was a terrible sin? Explain.

What happened to these people because of what they had done? (5:3-11)

It may be hard to understand why the punishment for these people was so severe when their sin didn't seem all that major. But we must remember that this is the first recorded sin in the formation of the church. These people were exhibiting greed (by holding back part of the money), pride (by taking more credit than they deserved), and lying (by trying so hard to cover up what they had done). But their worst sin was not against the other believers, but against God. They took lightly their part in building God's church. If they had not been punished for their sinful intentions, and if their plan had later been discovered, then it would have seemed that "crime pays" and that God isn't all that hard to fool. So they paid severely for their sin.

How did the apostles continue their ministry at this time? (5:12-16)

The jealous religious leaders tried to suppress the teaching of the apostles, but God was taking care of His people. What was one thing He did for them? (5:17-26)

Again a conflict flared up between the religious leaders and the followers of Jesus. The Jewish leaders were ready to have all of Jesus' followers killed, but one of their wiser members (a man named Gamaliel) made a suggestion. He had the apostles sent out and then addressed his peers. What recommendation did Gamaliel make? (5:33-39)

How did the religious leaders respond to Gamaliel's advice? (5:40)

How did Gamaliel's advice affect the followers of Jesus? (5:41-42)

JOURNEY INWARD

As you have seen, the period following Jesus' return to heaven was a turbulent time in one sense, but in another way it was very exciting. With the coming of the Holy Spirit on the day of Pentecost, a new era was begun in church history. Where the emphasis had previously been on the personal ministry of Jesus, the focus now shifts to the work of the Holy Spirit. And in these early years of the church, one issue keeps coming up—the emphasis on **integrity**.

As the Holy Spirit began to work through the ordinary disciples, it must have been a little difficult for them not to feel "special" or "chosen." But they kept insisting that they were just the same simple people. The only difference was that they were allowing God to work through them. Contrast the disciples with Ananias and Sapphira and you can see how important it is to maintain integrity in connection with your spiritual commitment.

Compare your level of spiritual integrity with that of the early disciples by answering the following questions.
(1) Even before the day of Pentecost, the disciples committed to follow Jesus' instructions to the letter and patiently wait in Jerusalem until something happened. Do you faithfully attend to the things you know Jesus wants you to do, or do you occasionally get impatient and do what *you* want to do? Give specific examples.

(2) When the disciples began to receive the power of the Holy Spirit and do miraculous things, they refused to take any credit for them-selves. Do you ever take a superior attitude toward others because you are a Christian and they aren't? Explain your answer.

(3) The early believers shared everything with each other so that no one was needy while others had an excess. How willing are you to share what you have with other Christians?

(4) The disciples also went outside their own circle of friends so they could proclaim the Gospel of Christ to people who hadn't yet heard (like the crippled beggar, for example). Do you feel uncomfortable when you get outside your circle of Christian friends, or do you regularly tell non-Christians about Jesus?

(5) When the disciples began to be persecuted because of their teachings, they steadfastly refused to change their story. When you receive resistance from others because of what you believe or what you express, do you ever try to take back what you have said? Do you immediately tone it down a little? Or do you boldly stick to your beliefs? Be specific.

(6) Ananias and Sapphira had no integrity. They tried to impress all their peers and still skim off some of the profits for themselves. And it is indeed dangerous to put on a religious front when you aren't really serious about what you're doing or saying. Do you ever do "religious" things more for show than from the heart? List as many examples as you can think of.

Now go back through all your answers and try to pick out the main areas where you might need to work on your integrity. Focus on those areas as you continue through this book.

Something else you might want to do before finishing this session is to think of a nickname for yourself that would address your weak area(s). For example, Joseph was such an encouragement to the disciples that they stopped calling him Joseph and instead called him Barnabas (which today might be interpreted "Mr. Encouragement"). So if you are having a problem with honesty, for example, you might give yourself the nickname "Honest (Your Name Here)" or "Faithful Frieda" or whatever. And after you come up with a nickname, spend the next week trying to live up to it. As you regularly remind yourself of your new name, you will also be reminded of the responsibility that goes along with it.

And by the way, it's also a good idea to give positive nicknames to your friends to remind them of their good qualities. Instead of going with the usual derogative nicknames like "Dog-Breath," "Pizza Face," "B.O.," and so forth, try to come up with something more positive (and more original) that will emphasize their noteworthy attributes. You've got to admit, if you are really smart but a little overweight, you might rather be known as Pat "Einstein" Palooka instead of Pat "Lardbottom" Palooka. Be creative and be sincere. Assign postitive nicknames for your friends below.

While you're testing your nicknames, don't forget to work on improving your level of integrity. Christianity is more than a role play to do while others are watching. It's a 24-hour-a-day commitment to act as Jesus would act in whatever situations you face. And while you may sometimes lose face or lose patience, you should make sure you never lose your integrity.

 KEY VERSE

"You will receive power when the Holy Spirit comes on you; and you will be My witnesses in Jerusalem, and in all Judea and Samaria, and to the ends of the earth" (Acts 1:8).

BLINDED BY THE LIGHT

(Acts 6—12)

Pauline was angry. No, she was more than angry. She was totally steamed. As student council vice president, she had been assigned to put together all the facts she could about changing the school mascot. And she had worked hard. She had collected options for new names. She had gotten cost estimates for replacing the current school signs (containing the old mascot) with new ones. She had found city business people willing to help fund the change and to promote the new school mascot. She had presented her plan brilliantly. And it had been voted down!

The issue was one that Pauline genuinely believed in, which was one of the reasons she was mad (though not the main reason). Frankly, she was sick and tired of her school being known as "The Home of the Fighting Squids." She didn't care if the school *did* overlook the ocean. She was fed up with cheers like, "Go, Squids, Go," and "Gimme an S, gimme a Q. . . ." (Whenever the cheerleaders got to the end of that cheer and yelled, "What have you got?" Pauline always wanted to shout back, "Bait!") *Anything* else would make a better mascot than a *squid.*

But the main things that had Pauline ticked off were the reasons her plan was voted down by the student council. The vote was 3 in favor and 5 against. Here's why the people voted no:

- Bobby Blotchface said his parents had put pressure on him. Bobby's grandfather had been a Fighting Squid. His mother and dad had both been Fighting Squids. And, confound it, why shouldn't Bobby be overjoyed to be a Fighting Squid too?
- Millie, the class treasurer, voted against changing because she was artistic and knew she would probably be involved with designing new school signs. She didn't really *want* to be a Fighting Squid either, but it was better than having to do all that extra work.
- Harold Chesterfield, III, the class president, hadn't really given any good reasons for voting no. He had been in favor of changing the mascot at first. But Pauline strongly suspected that he was jealous of all the hard work she had done (and all the attention she was likely to receive if her proposal were approved).
- A couple of other people just hadn't cared enough one way or the other to vote in favor of change. (Pauline wondered why those people had ever run for student council in the first place.)

And after working so hard for nothing, Pauline decided this was the last time she would ever waste *her* time trying to change things for the better. From now on, she would let someone else struggle to improve things.

Change comes hard for some people. And Pauline ran into many of the obstacles that prevent change: tradition, apathy, jealousy, laziness, convenience, and so forth. But perhaps Pauline's personal experience reveals one of the most tragic reasons not to attempt change—past failures. It's important not to let previous defeats or setbacks get in the way of much-needed change.

JOURNEY ONWARD

As you saw in the last session, the Jewish religious community had been undergoing some significant changes. Jesus had come to Earth, died, risen again, and ascended into heaven. The Holy Spirit had come down and the once-cowardly apostles were boldly proclaiming the Gospel throughout Jerusalem. The church was being started, and believers were sharing all they had with each other.

The "church" at this time had grown from the 11 remaining disciples to a group of about 120 (Acts 1:15), to 3,000 (2:41), to 5,000 (4:4). Naturally, that kind of rapid growth was bound to cause some problems—even with everyone working together. What was one of the first problems to surface? (6:1)

How did the apostles take care of the problem? (6:2-7)

One of the men they had selected was almost too good a choice. How did Stephen get in trouble with the religious authorities? (6:8-10)

What did the religious leaders do to incriminate Stephen? (6:11-14)

Would you like to have had the job of prosecuting Stephen?

When the high priest began to interrogate him, Stephen used the opportunity to review Jewish history for the religious leaders. He strung together the stories of Abraham, Isaac, Jacob, Joseph, Moses, David, and Solomon (7:1-50). What was Stephen leading up to? (7:51-53)

How did the Jewish leaders react to Stephen's accusations? (7:54)

What else happened to confirm that Stephen knew what he was talking about? (7:55-56)

But the hard-hearted religious authorities refused to even consider what Stephen was saying. They dragged him outside and began to stone him. What was Stephen's attitude as he died? (7:57-60)

Who was one of the observers at Stephen's death, and how did this person feel about Stephen's sentence? (7:58; 8:1)

What happened as a result of Stephen's trial and death? (8:1-3)

Stephen wasn't the only noteworthy person from the group of seven people appointed to help the apostles. Philip was another. (There was also a disciple named Philip, but this isn't the same man.) What kind of ministry did Philip have? (8:4-8)

A man named Simon saw Philip doing miraculous things and was fascinated by him. Why was Simon so interested in Philip? (8:9-11)

How did Simon respond to Philip's preaching? (8:12-13)

When the apostles in Jerusalem heard that the Samaritans were believing the Gospel, they sent Peter and John to check it out. What happened when Peter and John got to Samaria? (8:14-17)

What foolish request did Simon (the sorcerer) make of Peter and John that suggested that he might not be a true believer in Jesus? (8:18-25)

Meanwhile, Philip was still keeping busy. An angel had instructed him to go down a road that led into a desert, and of course Philip did what he was told. Whom did he meet on that road, and what was important about that person? (8:26-27)

[NOTE: A eunuch was a man who had had his sexual organs removed so he could serve female royalty without suspicion.]

What problem was this person having (besides going through life without his sexual organs)? (8:28-33)

How did Philip help him? (8:34-38)

As Philip's new friend rejoiced in his salvation, what happened to Philip? (8:39-40)

STOP IT, SAUL

While all this was going on, persecution continued for those who publicly professed to believe in Jesus. And one of the major persecutors was Saul, the young man who had tended to the coats of the people who had stoned Stephen. Since the center of opposition to Christianity seemed to be in Jerusalem, Saul had requested permission to go to other cities and bring believers back to Jerusalem as prisoners. He had received permission to go to Damascus for just such a mission. But something unexpected happened on the way to Damascus. What happened to Saul? (9:1-6)

What condition was Saul in when he finally arrived in Damascus? (9:7-9)

Before long there was another person who didn't feel too good either. God wanted to put Saul in touch with some of the Christians in Damascus, so He asked a man named Ananias to go find Saul. (This isn't the same Ananias from last session.) Put yourself in Ananias' place. He knew that Saul was coming to Damascus to arrest and persecute believers in Jesus. And now God was asking Ananias to go up to Saul and identify himself as a believer. What did Ananias do? (9:10-19)

It didn't take Saul long to change his attitude. But then, after a blinding revelation of who Jesus really is, it probably wouldn't take many of us too long to suspect that we were on the wrong track. What was one result of Saul's conversion to Christianity? (9:20-22)

What was another? (9:23-25)

When Saul returned to Jerusalem, he experienced the same problem of having all the believers mistrust him. This time it was Barnabas ("Mr. Encouragement") who took the first step and brought Saul to the disciples. And again, some of the traditional Jews tried to kill him. But he escaped back to his hometown of Tarsus (9:26-31).

DREAM FEAST

While this was going on, Peter was still doing miraculous things by the power of God, which attracted many people to his message of the Gospel. What did Peter do for a man named Aeneas? (9:32-35)

What did Peter do for a woman named Tabitha, or Dorcas? (9:36-42)

But Peter still had things to learn about God's plans for the structure of the church. He didn't know it, but God was going to call him to Caesarea. God used a man named Cornelius to summon Peter. What kind of person was Cornelius? (10:1-8)

Even while Cornelius' messengers were on their way to ask him to come, Peter had a vision. What did God show Peter? (10:9-16)

Keep in mind that Peter was a good Jew to whom the mere suggestion of eating an "unclean" animal was most offensive. Also keep in mind that Cornelius was a Gentile (non-Jew) who had no such feelings. Yet Cornelius was a devout, God-fearing man. While Peter was pondering his vision, the messengers from Cornelius arrived. Peter had them spend the night and he returned with them the next day. Cornelius explained why he had sent for Peter, and then asked Peter to say a few words (10:17-33).

Peter naturally used the opportunity to present the message of Jesus' death and resurrection. Even though Cornelius (and perhaps many of his friends) were good religious people, Peter presented the piece of the puzzle that they hadn't comprehended: Jesus Christ is Lord of all (10:34-43).

What effect did Peter's message have on Cornelius and those who were with him? (10:44-46)

What happened next? (10:47-48)

How much do you think Peter's vision had to do with his actions? Explain.

This was a significant action that Peter took. Up to this time, just about the only people who had joined the church and been baptized were Jewish people who knew the Scripture, who had been circumcised when they were eight days old, and who practiced all the traditions of the Jewish law. But Cornelius and his friends weren't Jewish, weren't circumcised, and had never been required to practice the Jewish traditions. As you might expect, when Peter went back to Jerusalem he had some explaining to do.

What was the attitude of the Jewish believers at first? (11:1-3)

After Peter explained (11:4-17), how did the Jewish believers respond? (11:18)

As the church went through its growing pains from the persecution in Jerusalem and began to spread out, most of the preaching was being done to Jews in the areas outside of Jerusalem. But some of the disciples went to a city called Antioch and began to teach the non-Jewish people about Jesus. Many people in Antioch believed the disciples' message and were converted. So the church sent who else but Barnabas ("Mr. Encouragement") to motivate the people to remain true to their new faith. Barnabas then sent for Saul to come help him. And at Antioch, a new name was given to the group of people who believed in Jesus. What were those people called from that time onward? (11:19-30)

Still the persecution of the church continued. King Herod had already killed one of Jesus' original disciples—James (the brother of John and one of the two that Jesus had nicknamed "Sons of Thunder"). The Jews were so pleased with Herod that he decided to do it again. This time he arrested Peter, put him in prison, and was going to have a public trial for him. How well was Peter guarded? (12:1-6)

Do you think Peter was afraid at this time? Explain your answer.

How did Peter get out of jail free? (12:7-11)

How would you have felt if you had been Peter in this situation?

The church people had been praying for Peter during his ordeal (12:5), and their prayers surely included the request that God would deliver him from prison. So how did these people react when Peter showed up at their door and told them he was free? (12:12-17)

What happened to the guards who had been watching Peter? (12:18-19)

The family of King Herod had done a lot to persecute Jesus and the church in their lifetimes. The grandfather of the King Herod in this passage was the King Herod who had killed all the baby boys in an attempt to eliminate Jesus as a child (Matthew 2:16). The father of the King Herod in our passage was the Herod who had killed John the Baptist to impress his party guests (Matthew 14:1-12) and had tried Jesus at Pilate's request. The King Herod in our passage had killed James (the apostle) and had tried to kill Peter. But the Herods' disregard for the will of God was about to catch up with them. What happened to this King Herod? (12:19-23)

How was all the persecution at this time affecting the church? (12:24)

 JOURNEY INWARD

From this account of the early church, and particularly from the stories of Peter's and Paul's visions, it's clear that we may occasionally need to learn to do things differently than we've always done them before. So now might be a good time to consider how you normally react to **change**.

But before you consider how you respond to change, spend a few minutes thinking about how you got to be the way you are. For example, you may know two kids with the same biological parents and the same upbringing, yet who are totally different. Obviously something besides genetics and environment has had an influence on one or both of them. Think of all the influences that have helped shape your character and attitudes and list them below.

Now go back and put a √ mark beside the three influences you think have had the most impact on you. Why do you think each of these things (or people) have been so influential?

Suppose for a moment that you had never come into contact with the three influences you just checked. How might your life be different now?

What are the three things you most need to change about yourself? Focus more on needs rather than wants. It's too easy to say, "I'd like to change by being (1) richer, (2) prettier, and (3) more powerful." But it might be legitimate to say that you need to change your attitude toward (1) money, (2) pride, and (3) prestige. Spend a couple of minutes and come up with your three most-needed changes. Write them below.

Now you need to ask yourself, "If I say I want to change for the better but haven't done it yet, why haven't I?" The answer may lie in the influences that you previously checked. After we form patterns of behavior, sometimes it's hard to break out of them and change. But we can encounter what psychologists call "significant events" that have a profound and longlasting effect on us, and that motivate us to change. A significant event can be positive (marriage, reading a book that dynamically influences your life, a religious conversion, etc.) or negative (the death of someone close, divorce, etc.).

Peter's vision was one such event that had a positive effect on him. He had been reared as a good Jew who would have nothing to do with Gentiles and even less with unclean foods. But God dealt with Peter in a powerful way and let him know clearly that it was time for him to change his attitudes. Perhaps God wants to show you that your feelings toward certain things or people are improper or outdated. Review your list of things that you feel you need to change and ask God to help you make those changes—no matter what it takes.

And by the way, this type of self-examination should be done regularly. It is true that Christians should show a degree of consistency in their lifestyles, but it is dangerous to become complacent or "stuck in a rut." Saul was a good religious person—or so he thought. But then he discovered that God had something better for him.

We should always be in search of the areas of our lives that need changing for the better. (It's like seeing your dentist twice a year to look for cavities. You may not have a problem, but it's still wise to do a thorough search.) God will reward you as you continue your struggle to mature as a Christian.

 **KEY VERSE**

"I now realize how true it is that God does not show favoritism but accepts men from every nation who fear Him and do what is right" (Acts 10:34).

ALL OPPOSED?

(Acts 13–16)

(1) You decide you want to learn to play the guitar because you really like the solo style of the lead guitarist of the Electric Buffaloes. So you talk your parents into buying you a pretty good second-hand instrument. After about a week, you can play the G, C, D, E, A, and almost the F chords. But then you discover that a lot of your favorite songs have minor keys and sevenths and assorted chords that you couldn't play if you had three hands to hold the correct frets. What do you do?

_____ (A) Keep practicing and doing finger exercises until you can play all the right chords and have mastered the guitar.

_____ (B) Try to talk your parents into letting you take lessons.

_____ (C) Put the guitar in your closet, expecting to take it up again, oh, someday. Meanwhile you notice how good the lead singer of the Purple Watermelons looks as he does his saxophone solo, and you begin to put together your speech to convince you parents to get you a sax.

_____ (D) Just think, *Oh, this is too hard,* and forget about the guitar (and music lessons) altogether.

(2) You go out for one of the sports teams at your school. The truth is that you want to look good in the uniform for all the rest of your friends. But when you begin to show up for practices, you discover that most of the time is spent running laps and doing rigorous exercises. Then in the first game you get paired against an opponent who looks like a mutant offspring of the Incredible Hulk. What do you do?

_____ (A) Decide that your social status is fine even without membership on that particular sports team.

_____ (B) Explain to your coach that it's just too hard to do all that work for a little bit of playing time, and that sweating messes up your expensive haircut.

_____ (C) Stay on the team and do absolutely as little as possible just to get by.

_____ (D) Tough it out and get your flabby body into shape by pushing hard on the exercises and continuing to take on fierce opponents.

(3) You have always wanted to be a journalist. You watch the news every night with admiration for the people who put the stories together, even while they're happening. You figure that's the life for you. But the problem is your writing teacher. He just seems to have it in for you— asking you the hardest questions in class, giving you C's that you thought should have been A's, tossing you the toughest assignments, etc. You figure you'll have to take at least two more classes under this teacher to graduate, and you're not sure you want to be a journalist that much. What do you do?

_____ (A) Decide that being a garbage collector probably isn't really as bad as you've always imagined.

_____ (B) Stick with the class you're in and hope the teacher gets transferred to another school before you have another class with him.

_____ (C) Accept the teacher's hard assignments and grading system as a challenge that must be overcome.

_____ (D) Tell him that he's just being too hard on you. Surely Walter Cronkite, Dan Rather, David Brinkley, Ted Koppel, and the others didn't have to suffer like you are having to do.

(4) Name your own circumstances. What's a current situation that you face where you encounter a lot of opposition? And what are you planning to do about it?

In case you haven't figured it out yet, your life is going to be full of situations similar to the ones just described. You will always have a certain amount of opposition (from somewhere!) that stands in the way of peaceful existence. And how you handle that opposition will determine how well you can cope with the little setbacks of life.

 JOURNEY ONWARD

This session will focus on a few people who went through a tremendous amount of opposition (both internal and external) in order to help the church grow. The focus is no longer on Peter. It has shifted to Saul, and from now on you will be hearing much about how he will suffer (voluntarily) for the cause of Christ—for which he originally made others suffer (involuntarily).

The Holy Spirit directed the church leaders to allow Saul to tour a number of cities and preach the Gospel. Who else was called to accompany Saul? (Acts 13:1-3)

Who was the third person that these two people invited along? (12:25; 13:4-5)

Their first stop was the island of Cyprus. What opposition did they face there? (13:6-8)

How did Saul deal with this opposition? (13:9-12)

Note (in Acts 13:9) that Saul had another name, by which he is more well known. "Saul" was more of a traditional Jewish name (remember the first king of Israel?), while "Paul" was more common among Greeks and Romans. As Saul began to minister to the non-Jewish people, he was more commonly referred to as Paul.

After their stop at Cyprus, the three travelers set out for a place called Antioch in the area of Pisidia. This city was a Roman colony that was northwest of the city of Antioch where the disciples were first called Christians. But on their way, the trio became a duo. Why? (13:13)

On the Sabbath, Paul and Barnabas went to the synagogue and were invited to speak. Paul stood and gave a summary of Jewish religious history, but added the part about how Jesus had come to fulfill all that had been established by the Law and the Prophets (13:14-41, esp. vv. 32-33). What kind of response to his message did Paul receive? (13:42-44)

What did the local Jews do when they saw the kind of response that Paul was getting? (13:45-50)

How did Paul and Barnabas respond to this opposition? (13:51-52)

The next stop on the tour was Iconium. The crowd who heard Paul speak was divided between those who believed him and those who didn't. Paul ignored his critics at first and continued to speak boldly. But then the opposition intensified. How? (14:1-5)

How did Paul and Barnabas handle this opposition? (14:6-7)

The next city on Paul's route was Lystra. In this town Paul healed a crippled man who had been lame from birth, and the response he received from the crowds was something else! What did the people there assume about Paul and Barnabas? (14:8-13)

What things did Paul and Barnabas do to point out that the people's assumption was incorrect? (14:14-18)

Even though Paul and Barnabas weren't able to change the crowd's way of thinking, other people *were*. Some of the jealous Jewish people who had disagreed with Paul in Iconium and Antioch had followed them to Lystra, and had eventually persuaded the Lystrans to listen to them. As a result, what happened to Paul? (14:19-20)

The people in the next city, Derbe, responded more favorably. Many of them became disciples. Then, in spite of the opposition Paul and Barnabas had met in the towns along their route, they decided to retrace their steps and go back through those same places on their way home. What did they do this time through? (14:21-25)

And after all they had experienced, they were able to give a good report when they got back to their starting point in Antioch (14:26-28). But it wasn't long before conflict arose within the church at Antioch. What was the issue that was dividing the church members? (15:1-2)

This issue was no small disagreement, so a council was scheduled in Jerusalem where people could assemble and discuss the matter. Summarize the statements made by the following people:

- The party of the Pharisees (15:5)—

- Peter (15:6-11)—

- Paul and Barnabas (15:12)—

When these people had spoken, a decision was made by James. (This James was the half-brother of Jesus, being one of the sons of Mary and

Joseph. James the apostle had already been put to death by King Herod.) What was James' decision concerning the uncircumcised believers? (15:13-21)

A letter was drafted detailing the terms of the decision and was delivered to Antioch by Paul, Barnabas, and two other leaders—Judas (Barsabbas) and Silas. The contents of the letter are recorded in Acts 15:23-29. What was the response to the letter in Antioch? (15:30-35)

THREE'S A CROWD
But the internal conflict between the church members wasn't over yet. A problem arose between Paul and Barnabas, of all people. What was the issue? (15:36-41)

Who do you think was right, Paul or Barnabas? Explain your answer.

From this point on, Barnabas and John Mark do not appear in the Book of Acts. But the tension between Paul and them didn't last forever. In Paul's later letters, he had good things to say about both Barnabas and Mark. However, at this time Paul recruited a new traveling companion—Silas.

Paul and Silas went to Derbe and Lystra again, where they found a young disciple Paul wanted to have travel with them. Who was he? (16:1-2)

What was Paul's recommendation for this person before he went out to preach with Paul and Silas? Why? (16:3-5)

Paul intended to go to some places he hadn't visited on his first journey. As it turned out, he *did* see some new territory. But it wasn't the route he had planned to take. How did Paul know which direction to go? (16:6-10)

(By the way, if you've been reading very closely up to this point, you might notice a subtle change of perspective in this historic account in the Book of Acts. Until now, the writer has descibed the events in terms of "they" did this and "they" did that. But when Paul, Silas, and Timothy got to Troas, the point of view changes. It becomes, *"We* got ready," "God had called *us* to preach," *"We* put out to sea," and so forth. It is very likely that at this time Luke joined Paul for a while.)

Paul and his companions spent several days in the city of Philippi, a Roman colony in Macedonia. Who met Paul there and believed his message, and what was this person's trade? (16:11-15)

While in Philippi, Paul removed a spirit from a slave girl. But his good deed wasn't appreciated by the girl's owners. Why not? (16:16-19)

What kind of opposition did Paul and Silas face? (16:20-24)

How did they deal with this opposition? (16:25)

What was the result of their perseverance throughout this opposition? (16:26-34)

What the Philippians hadn't known was that Paul was a Roman citizen and had certain rights (including the right not to be beaten without a trial). So when the jailer came to release Paul and Silas from prison, what happened? (16:35-40)

We'll leave Paul in Philippi for this session and continue from there next time. But before moving on, reflect for a while on Paul's journeys so far.

 JOURNEY INWARD

It may be hard for you to relate to some of the problems that Paul was going through—stonings, beatings, being followed around by hostile crowds, and so forth. But then, you probably have some other things in common with him. Perhaps you have taken a stand on a Christian or moral issue, even though you were in the minority. Maybe you've tried to talk to someone about Christianity, only to be ridiculed and rejected. So for whatever situations you're facing, it might be good to take another quick look at Paul's life to get some clues on how to handle **opposition.**

A good way to start is to list all the situations where you face opposition from others. Put some time into recalling each of the recent times you've wanted to do something constructive, only to have your good intentions slammed back in your face. Write the situations below.

Now keep your list in mind as you review the various ways Paul responded to opposition. For example, when Paul faced opposition from the people in Pisidian Antioch, he reacted to it by "shaking the dust from his feet" and just walking away (13:51). Should you respond to any of the situations you've just listed by simply walking away from them? If so, mark the situation(s) off of your first list and write them below.

In other situations, it wasn't enough for Paul to walk away—he *ran* (14:5-7). He knew he was up against so many cold-blooded, hardhearted people that it would be useless (and stupid) to resist. In your own situations, do you need to flee from your opposition (for now) to give you time to calm down and focus on more constructive areas? If so, mark those situations off your first list and record them below.

Sometimes Paul knew he should neither walk nor run from his opposition. (For instance, he had the perfect opportunity to escape from the Philippian prison, but he chose to stay.) Cross off any applicable situations on your list and put them in the space below.

God sometimes allows His people to undergo discomfort at the hands of their adversaries. But at other times He provides exceptional power to silence the opponents of His truth. For instance, when Paul was accosted by Elymas the sorcerer, he claimed the power of God to get rid of the obstacle. God temporarily blinded Elymas in order to show all who were watching that Paul was speaking the truth (13:6-12). If you have any items on your list that you haven't crossed off yet, perhaps you need to ask God for a special amount of strength and courage. Write these situations below and cross them off your original list.

We need to consider one other possibility. If you have situations on your list that haven't yet been crossed off (or this may even apply to some that *have* already been crossed off), you should ask yourself: "Could I be facing this situation because *I'm* wrong?" If you are doing things for selfish reasons or that aren't really what God wants done, you will surely face opposition. And such opposition might be a clue that you should change your attitudes and actions.

Spend a few minutes at this point being honest with God about all these situations in which you've been encountering opposition. Ask Him to show you how He would have you respond to each matter that has come to your mind. Follow His leading in the areas where you may be the source of opposition. And prayerfully prepare yourself for the opposition that you are likely to face in the upcoming weeks and months. You'll never be free from opposition (unless, of course, you want to live as a hermit in a cave away from the rest of the world). But you *can* learn to keep moving forward in the face of opposition. So get moving.

 **KEY VERSE**

"We must go through many hardships to enter the kingdom of God" (Acts 14:22).

PUT SOME WIT IN YOUR WITNESS

(Acts 17—21:36)

Something unusual happened to Bill one night just as he was finishing his bedtime prayers.

BILL: For Thine is the kingdom, and the power, and the glory forever. Amen.

VOICE: [*Gently*] Bill?

BILL: [*Looks around, somewhat astonished*]

VOICE: [*More forceful*] Bill!

BILL: W-who's there?

VOICE: This is the Lord. Weren't you just talking to Me?

BILL: No, not me. I was just saying the Lord's Prayer. [*Pause*] Oh, I get it. The Lord's Prayer, and You're the Lord.

VOICE: That's right.

BILL: W-what do You want with me?

VOICE: I have a job I want you to do.

BILL: Are You sure You have the right person?

VOICE: I'm never wrong. You are just the person for the mission I have in mind.

BILL: [*To himself*] Oh, no. I've heard what kinds of stuff God makes His missionaries do. I bet He wants me to go to Zululand or Tierra del Fuego or some other awful place.

VOICE: I want you to visit your friend John next door.

BILL: [*Continuing to ignore voice*] I'll probably have to wear polyester clothes and teach a bunch of cannibals to eat vegetables.

VOICE: I want you to play golf with him a couple of times each week.

BILL: I'll have to eat locusts and roots and iguanas.

VOICE: Then go out for pizza and ice cream.

BILL: God probably wants me to do this because I've been rotten.

VOICE: I want you to do this because I can trust you.

BILL: He knows how much I hate snakes and spiders and bugs and piranhas.

VOICE: I know how much you love to play golf.

BILL: All for a bunch of people I've never seen.

VOICE: After all, John *is* your best friend.

BILL: And I'll probably have to learn to preach, lead hymns, dig wells, and build churches.

VOICE: And all I want you to do is to invite him to go to church with you. He doesn't know much about Me.

BILL: I'm sorry, but I'm just not cut out to be a missionary. Why doesn't God ever ask me to do something I like to do?

VOICE: [*Slight sigh*] Why don't people ever listen when I talk to them?

If your idea of missions or telling others about Jesus is anything like Bill's, pay attention as you go through this session and see how the Apostle Paul responded to the challenges of telling others about Jesus

JOURNEY ONWARD

You may remember that we left Paul and Silas in Philippi, where they had just gotten out of prison. (Timothy and Luke were also in Philippi with them.) While they had been eager to continue to spread the Gospel throughout Europe, they had certainly had more than their share of opposition. We'll see in this session whether or not they were going to let their persecutors get to them.

After Philippi, Paul's next significant stop was Thessalonica. Paul spoke in the synagogue and several people believed his message. What groups of people were beginning to believe in Jesus' sacrificial death and resurrection? (17:1-4)

But Paul and Silas were still victims of opposition. What kind of opposition did they face in Thessalonica? (17:5-9)

How did Paul and Silas react to this opposition? (17:10)

In the next town, Berea, the people reacted a little differently than anywhere Paul had stopped before. What was the Berean response to Paul's teaching? (17:11-12)

Again, opposition forced Paul to leave. But since Paul seemed to be the focus of all the opposition, he was escorted to safety while Silas and Timothy stayed in Berea a little longer. (Timothy may have remained in Philippi a while and perhaps had just caught up with the group at this point.) In the meantime, Paul went ahead to Athens. What was his first impression of the city? (17:16-17)

Paul's comments in the synagogue captured the attention of several people, because the people in Athens welcomed new ideas and intellectual debate. So Paul was invited to speak in the Areopagus ("Hill of Ares," or "Mars' Hill"). This was a large civic meeting area. And the people were eager to hear what Paul had to say (17:18-21). How did Paul introduce the subject of Christianity as he addressed this group of people? (17:22-23)

From his introduction, Paul moved on to describe God in terms of Creator, Father, Saviour, and Judge. His words must have been unique to a culture whose daily routine included many different gods. Read Acts 17:24-31 and write down the things Paul said to indicate he was talking to Greek people who knew nothing about his God (as opposed to Jewish people in the synagogue).

What kind of response did Paul get from his Greek audience? (17:32-34)

From Athens, Paul moved on to Corinth. There he met a couple with whom he had something in common. Who were the people, and what was their common interest with Paul? (18:1-4)

A NEW DIRECTION
It was in Corinth that Paul's ministry took a different turn. How did Paul shift his emphasis, and what was responsible for the change? (18:5-6)

Paul didn't go far when he left the synagogue—just next door. How was his message received there? (18:7-8)

How was Paul sure he was doing what God wanted him to do? (18:9-11)

Paul actually got to put down roots in Corinth for a while. He stayed a year and a half, teaching them the Word of God. But Paul's popularity was still annoying to some of the Jews. This time, instead of beating him up or running him out of town, they decided to take legal action against him. Yet the Roman guy in charge (Gallio) didn't think the Jews' accusations against Paul were even worthy of his time, and he tossed them out of his court (18:12-17).

When Paul finally left Corinth, he took with him his new friends, Priscilla and Aquila. He had previously taken some kind of vow (no one knows exactly why). One of the conditions of the vow was that he would not have his hair cut. Apparently his vow was fulfilled at this point because he got a haircut before he sailed for his next destination—Ephesus.

Paul went straight to the synagogue and "reasoned with the Jews" (18:19). How was he received by the Jews in Ephesus? (18:20-21)

Paul was apparently in a hurry to get back to Jerusalem, because he quickly set sail for Caesarea, a coastal town near Jerusalem. When he arrived he "greeted the church" and then moved on to Antioch. After a short stay in Antioch, Paul left for a third missionary journey. What was his purpose for going on this third tour? (18:23)

While Paul was traveling, another person was making a name for himself in Ephesus and Achaia. His name was Apollos. (Remember the name; you'll hear more of him before you finish this book.) What kind of person was Apollos? (18:24-28)

When Paul arrived at Ephesus, what was he able to do for some of the newer believers there? (19:1-7)

How was Paul received by the Jewish leaders in Ephesus? (19:8-10)

In spite of Paul's rejection by the religious leaders, how was he able to prove that he spoke with authority? (19:11-12)

Some of the local people tried to imitate Paul's miracles just by saying the right words, as if Paul were using some kind of magic spell to cast out evil spirits. How did this practice backfire on some of them? (19:13-16)

When the townspeople saw the consequences of misusing the name of Jesus, what were the results? (19:17-20)

After seeing these things take place, Paul decided he should head back toward Jerusalem. After that, he had a desire to go to Rome (19:21-22). But before he could get out of Ephesus, what happened that threatened to postpone his departure? (19:23-28)

Do you think these people were primarily concerned with their religious beliefs toward the goddess Artemis? Or do you think they were mainly worried that their source of income was being threatened? Explain your answer.

What actions did these angry business people take? (19:28-34)

How was a full-scale riot avoided? (19:35-41)

ON THE ROAD AGAIN

Paul was then able to say his good-byes and move on. He went on to Macedonia where he was going to set sail. But he decided to double back and retrace his route through Macedonia instead. Why? (20:1-3)

By this time, Paul had several traveling companions (20:4). And at Philippi it appears that Luke hooked up with Paul again. (The point of view again becomes "we" and "us.") The next stop was Troas, where something rather unusual happened. What happened that perhaps we should remember the next time we're tempted to nap during the Sunday sermon? (20:7-9)

What did Paul do to remedy the crisis at hand? (20:10-12)

Paul continued on his way to Jerusalem, but before he got too far he sent for the leaders of the church in Ephesus. He reminded them of the sincerity of his ministry among them, and they told them something that distressed them. What did Paul want them to know? (20:22-25)

What did Paul warn them about? (20:26-31)

How did the Ephesian elders respond to Paul's farewell? (20:32-38)

As Paul continued toward Jerusalem, what was one warning he received to indicate that it might not be in his best interest to go there? (21:1-6)

But Paul was determined to continue. On the way, Paul and his traveling companions stayed at Philip's home. By this time, Philip wasn't the only one of his household who was active in ministry. What other family members of Philip's were known for their spiritual gifts? (21:7-9)

What else happened to Paul as a warning of what lay ahead for him in Jerusalem? (21:10-11)

How did Paul respond to this warning? (21:12-16)

What was the first thing Paul did when he got to Jerusalem? (21:17-19)

Then he was called upon to clear up a misunderstanding. What rumors had been spreading about Paul that were incorrect? (21:20-21)

What did Paul do to help resolve the misunderstanding? (21:22-26)

But before Paul could even complete his seven-day commitment, he was spotted by several Jews from Asia. They accused Paul of taking a non-Jewish person into their temple, which was strictly forbidden (and which, by the way, was an unfounded charge). These Asian Jews enlisted the help of the local Jews to seize Paul. What did they want to do to him? (21:27-31)

What kept Paul from suffering the full punishment they had in mind for him? (21:31-32)

What happened to Paul instead? (21:33-36)

The next session will take Paul through a series of legal trials. In the meantime, we'll leave him in the protective custody of the Roman Empire. It will be a somber note as we consider the potential consequences of sharing our beliefs with others.

JOURNEY INWARD

You probably hear a lot these days about the importance of **telling others about Jesus.** Many Christians place a heavy emphasis on sharing their faith with others, and rightly so. The last instruction Jesus left His disciples before ascending into heaven was to "go and make disciples of all nations" (Matthew 28:19). And after reading this far through the Book of Acts, you've seen how quickly the church has grown due to the efforts of a relatively few people who were willing to tell others about Jesus.

From this session we can discover that there are some right and wrong ways to talk to others about Jesus. Work your way through the following observations, and then you'll have an opportunity to make some additional observations of your own.

OBSERVATION #1—*Telling others about Jesus should be a priority in a Christian's life.* The last session showed the many ways in which Paul and Silas faced opposition as they traveled. Yet this session continues the story by showing their insistence on continuing to be witnesses for God's good news of salvation. Is sharing your faith a regular part of your life? And if so, how is it affected when you face opposition? Be specific.

OBSERVATION #2—*God will direct you to people who are willing to listen.* Paul faced a lot of opponents in many of the places he went. But when he got to Berea, he found people willing to check out what he was telling them. Do you fear telling others about Jesus because you've had one or two bad experiences? If so, who do you know who is like the Bereans—people who will seriously consider what you say about Christianity? List those people below.

OBSERVATION #3—*Don't waste a lot of time talking to deaf ears.*
When you find people who are willing to listen, focus your time with
them. Yes, the love of God is available to everyone. But some people
simply won't be ready to accept it. Just as Paul shifted his emphasis
from the Jews to the Gentiles, you may need to go outside your regular
circle of friends to find people eager to hear about Christianity. What
activities are wasting your time—time that you could use to share what
God has done for you?

OBSERVATION #4—*Make the most of the opportunities God provides.*
When Paul found an altar dedicated "to an unknown God," he immediately recognized it as an opportunity to try to make the true God known
to his listeners. What are some opportunities you have had recently
that might have led into a discussion of spiritual things with a little transition on your part? What possibilities do you expect to have during the
next week? Think hard and be specific.

OBSERVATION #5—*Don't rely too much on formulas.* The seven
sons of Sceva thought they had found a secret way to make things happen, but they discovered they were very wrong. Even today some
people get caught up in a rigid, memorized, never-changing method for
approaching others with the Gospel message. Think of some ways that
you can prevent your method(s) of sharing your faith from getting into a
rut. Write them below.

OBSERVATION #6—*Christians aren't the only people who are "witnesses."* If you don't get involved with sharing your faith for God, others
are likely to recruit your non-Christian friends for ungodly causes.
Most people have an interest in spiritual things. But if they don't hear
about the truth of God, they are likely to become involved in cults, false

religions, or other organizations that are a poor substitute for a personal relationship with Jesus. Even in Paul's day, he faced competition. That's why he warned the Ephesians to be on their guard for false teachers—even from within their own church (Acts 20:30-31). Whom do you know who distorts the truth of God, and how do they do so?

OTHER OBSERVATIONS—(List the other things you want to remember from this session in the space below.)

It's important to keep in mind that God doesn't hold us accountable for the responses of the people we talk to. Paul would have had a pretty lousy batting average if he had been evaluated according to the percentage of people who believed out of all those who heard his testimony. But God *does* expect us to tell other people about Him, and He *will* hold us responsible for our willingness to share our faith with others. It's up to you to tell others what God has done for you. From that point on, it's between God and those people.

Your witness to others doesn't have to be witless. In fact, it takes quite a sharp wit to recognize and capitalize on the opportunities God sends your way. The role of a witness is to explain what he or she has observed. And if God is active in your life, that really shouldn't be all that difficult. But if you're out of touch with God, or scared, or shy, take a few minutes now to express your feelings to Him. He will provide whatever you need to move on from there.

KEY VERSE

"I consider my life worth nothing to me, if only I may finish the race and complete the task the Lord Jesus has given me—the task of testifying to the Gospel of God's grace" (Acts 20:24).

TRIED, TRIED AGAIN

(Acts 21:37—28)

You and a friend are set for a day in the park—Frisbee in hand and sack lunch in the car. But before you can toss the Frisbee back and forth three times, a small boy approaches you and wants help. It seems that he has a big test on long division the following Monday and he has no clue how to do the problems. You'd rather not get involved with his long division problems, but he has such a pathetic look on his face that you decide to help him. Yet no sooner have you gone through a couple of examples than a man comes toward the three of you, accompanied by two policemen.

One of the policemen explains that the man is the boy's father, who doesn't want anyone interfering with his child's education. The father had told the boy to figure out the solutions on his own, and had left him to accomplish his task. But more important, the father has asked the police to have you arrested for contributing to the education of a minor. The police try to talk him out of pressing charges, but the man is insistent. At this point, what would you do?

_____ Grab the father by the collar and shout, "Don't be ridiculous! There's no such offense as 'Contributing to the education of a minor.' I think you've been watching too many Perry Mason reruns, you legal nitwit."

_____ Ignore the man and continue to help the kid until the father takes him away (or the police take you away).

_____ Reason with the police and get them to release you on your own recognizance until you can get your parents involved and get the whole matter cleared up.

_____ Beg, grovel, or bribe—do anything to prevent having to go to the police station and possibly on to jail.

Now suppose the worst happens and the police take you in. At the station you discover that the man has connections at City Hall and usually gets whatever he wants. To make things worse, there's nobody home at your house—a fact you discover with your one phone call. Now what do you do?

_____ Enlist all the felons in the surrounding cells to join you in a sing-along.

_____ Keep reminding your guards that they have absolutely no legal right to hold you, using the phrase "false arrest" as many times as possible.

_____ Plan out all the details of a surefire escape plan.

_____ Shamelessly plead with whoever will listen to help you contact your parents or friends or anyone who might help you get out.

And while we're pretending, imagine that you discover your parents have just left for an extended European vacation. (They simply forgot to mention it to you.) In the meantime, your assigned attorney says she can get you released if you go ahead and sign a document admitting that you were completely at fault in the "park incident." She's sure she can have you cleared later. How would you respond?

_____ Rip up the document and boldly send it to the judge in one of the envelopes from your new "Prison Inmate Collection" of stationery.

_____ Politely say, "No thanks," and calmly explain that there's a principle involved here which your conscience simply cannot overlook.

_____ Quickly sign the paper and run like a bandit.

_____ Weep openly and kiss the feet of your lawyer many times before you sign the paper and run like a bandit.

Actually, most of us can only imagine what we might do in similar circumstances. Sometimes we're really brave when talking about what we would do in a difficult or unfair situation. We envision ourselves giving blood without wincing, getting cavities filled without squirming, and asking a new person on a date without getting sweaty palms. But when we actually find ourselves in those circumstances, we wince, squirm, and sweat like a horse.

 JOURNEY ONWARD

Paul, as you have seen, had no problem with shyness. In this session we'll see that he faced several situations much like the opening illustration in this session. He was accused of breaking the law and was arrested, when all he had done was tell people about Jesus. And instead of retreating when others tried to push an issue, Paul often pushed right back and made sure that everyone knew (beyond a doubt) where he stood. He never backed down from proclaiming the Gospel. Paul wouldn't let a simple little legal trial (or two or three) change his mission in the least.

You may want to read Acts 21:27-36 and review the events leading up to Paul's arrest. Simply put, he had been accused by foreign Jews of taking a non-Jewish person into the temple—an act that was against Jewish religious law. Paul's accusers were violent and were trying to kill him, but their plans were thwarted by a patrol of Roman soldiers. Paul was arrested and held until the Romans could determine the facts of the case.

But Paul didn't sit and twiddle his thumbs until justice could be served. What request did Paul make of the Roman soldiers? (21:37)

The soldiers were a little wary of Paul. They suspected he might be an Egyptian terrorist leader (which also might explain the two chains that had been placed on him [21:33]). But after Paul explained who he was and where he was from, he was allowed to speak.

Most of us in this situation would probably be quick to deliver the old Hey-wait-a-minute-you've-got-the-wrong-guy speech. But after he had everyone's attention, what did Paul do? (21:40—22:21)

What kind of response did Paul receive from the crowd? (22:22)

What were the Roman soldiers planning to do to Paul? (22:23-24)

Just as the sentence of the Roman commander was about to be carried out, Paul asked a simple little question. What was it? (22:25)

How did Paul's question affect the carrying out of his punishment? (22:26-29)

Up until this point, the Roman soldiers hadn't realized that Paul was a legitimate Roman citizen. In fact, Paul had been born a citizen while some of the others present had had to purchase a title of citizenship (which didn't come cheap). And one of Paul's rights as a citizen guaranteed that he would not be punished in one of the more humiliating ways reserved for noncitizens (beating with rods, crucifixion, and so forth). The soldiers realized that they had already treated Paul more severely than they should have. But the Roman commander still needed to know what Paul had done to aggravate the Jews so much. The next day he scheduled a time for Paul to speak to the Jewish Sanhedrin. When Paul began to talk, he got only one sentence out before he was interrupted. What was his lead-off statement? (23:1)

As soon as Paul made his first statement, the high priest gave an order concerning Paul. What did Ananias want done? (23:2)

How did Paul respond to the order of the high priest? (23:3)

Paul claimed that he didn't recognize that Ananias was the high priest. Some people suggest that Paul's comment may have been tongue-in-cheek (something to the effect of, "You *can't* be the high priest. You just told that person to punch me in the mouth, which would be against the law.") But Paul wasn't finished. He knew that the Sanhedrin was composed of both Pharisees (who believed in the resurrection of the dead) and Sadducees (who didn't believe in resurrection). What statement did Paul make? (23:6)

What was the effect of his statement? (23:7-10)

Roman soldiers were sent into the fray to ensure Paul's safety, and they whisked him away to spend another night in protective custody. You might think that Paul would be getting a little discouraged by this time. But he still had his desire to go to Rome. What bit of encouragement did Paul receive in this regard? (23:11)

Yet this bit of good news was soon tempered with the discovery of some bad news. What bad news did Paul get word of? (23:12-16)

How did Paul avoid this latest plot of the Jews? (23:17-24)

GOING TO THE GOVERNOR

A letter was written to Felix, the governor of Judea, explaining why Paul had suddenly been sent to his jurisdiction (23:25-30). What happened to Paul after his transfer? (23:31-35)

The high priest, some of the Jewish elders, and a lawyer named Tertullus traveled to Caesarea to prosecute Paul, and all the facts and accusations were spelled out for Felix (24:1-21). How did Felix respond to the proceedings? (24:22-23)

Why didn't Felix attempt a rapid settlement? (24:24-26)

How did Felix finally avoid making any decision at all? (24:27)

As soon as the new governor hit town, Paul's accusers were there to present their charges against Paul. Based on their proposal to Governor Festus, they must not have felt like they had a strong legal case against Paul. What was their "Plan B" to get rid of Paul? (25:1-3)

Festus refused their proposal because he wanted to be in on Paul's trial himself. Again the Jews brought their charges against Paul (25:4-7). Again Paul stuck to his defense. What did Paul keep insisting? (25:8)

Festus asked Paul if he would be willing to return to Jerusalem (where he had been tried originally) to stand trial there. What was Paul's answer? (25:9-12)

A few days later Festus was visited by King Agrippa, one of the main Roman leaders. Agrippa was accompanied by Bernice, his sister (and according to the rumor of the time, his lover as well). Festus and Agrippa started discussing business, and before long the subject of Paul's imprisonment came up. Agrippa expressed an interest in hearing what Paul had to say, so Festus set up a meeting for the next day (25:13-22). The mood of the gathering was one of "great pomp" (25:23) and included lots of important people.

King Agrippa encouraged Paul to speak freely. Paul began with a tactful address to Agrippa (26:1-3) followed by a brief explanation of why he was under arrest (26:4-8). Then what did Paul tell that group of very important people? (26:9-23)

At this point in Paul's speech, Festus interrupted him. What accusation did Festus make about Paul? (26:24)

Paul denied the accusation and then shifted the focus of attention to King Agrippa. When Paul started to get personal about spiritual things, how did Agrippa sidestep the issue somewhat? (26:25-28)

What was Paul's desire for those who were listening to him? (26:29)

What did his audience think about Paul? (26:30-32)

TO ROME—THE LONG WAY
The time finally came for Paul to be transported to Rome for his trial before Caesar. He and some other prisoners were placed on a ship and off they sailed. What kind of relationship did Paul have with Julius, the centurion in charge of the prisoners? (27:1-3)

Paul and his shipmates didn't have a smooth trip. They sailed against the wind the whole way. In fact, they were trying to travel at the very end of the year's sailing season, which ended five days after the Day of Atonement (the "Fast" that Luke refers to in 27:9). The seas were just too rough beyond that point (in late September or October). And during this difficult time, Paul shared a prophecy that the others didn't really want to hear. What did Paul predict? (27:9-10)

The people who ran the ship disregarded Paul's warning. They wanted to get to Phoenix, a harbor in Crete where they could spend the winter. What spoiled their plans? (27:13-15)

What happened then? (27:16-20)

Paul then revealed another prophecy. What good news and bad news did he have for his traveling companions? (27:21-26)

How did the sailors discover they were in trouble? (27:27-28)

Some of the sailors apparently didn't believe what Paul had predicted. What was their plan, and why didn't it work? (27:29-32)

Even though Paul was a prisoner, he seemed to be in control of the situation. What practical things did he do to encourage the others? (27:33-38)

During the shipwreck, how did Paul's friendship with the centurion pay off? (27:39-44)

After everyone had safely reached the island of Malta, they were welcomed by the people there. And Paul quickly made an impression on them. How? (28:1-6)

How else did Paul endear himself to the islanders? (28:7-10)

ROME AT LAST
How did Paul finally get to Rome? (28:11-15)

How was Paul allowed to live as a prisoner in Rome? (28:16)

Paul called together the Jewish leaders who were in Rome and explained the circumstances by which he had come there (28:17-20).

How was he received by the local Jewish leaders? (28:21-22)

How was he received by the Jewish people in Rome? (28:23-28)

How long did Paul stay in Rome? (28:30-31)

Although the historical account of Acts doesn't provide the end of Paul's story, most people agree that he was probably released from his Roman imprisonment. Some of Paul's later letters suggest that he was no longer in Rome, and tradition says that Paul eventually went to Spain. But for now, let's focus on what we know for sure about Paul.

 JOURNEY INWARD

Throughout the Book of Acts, Paul has stood as a bold, dynamic example of what one person is capable of doing if he or she will put total trust in Jesus. And so far in this book, you've had the opportunity to evaluate your own level of integrity, your ability to handle change and opposition, and your willingness to speak out for Jesus. As you complete the Book of Acts, spend a little time focusing on something that ties all these areas together. Think for a while now about **commitment.**

To get started, complete the following sentences:

- I would define commitment as . . .

- I know someone is committed to me when he or she . . .

- I spend most of my free time . . .

- I usually keep my word except when . . .

- Three words that define my commitment to God are . . .

- The "little" sins in my life that might suggest I need to strengthen my commitment to God are . . .

- The things I've done in the past 24 hours that would allow other people to see my commitment to God are . . .

- One thing that destroys a commitment to someone else is . . .

- When I'm doing things I've committed myself to do, I'm usually thinking . . .

- The main difference between my level of commitment and Paul's level of commitment is . . .

Obviously the topic of commitment is so broad that it would be hard to go into great detail here. But your completion of the previous sentences should help you narrow it down somewhat. Your commitments are reflected by your relationships with your friends, the way you spend your time, your attitudes, and so forth. It doesn't take an Albert

Einstein to look at someone for a short time and figure out what he or she is committed to.

Don't you think it would have been impossible to hang around the Apostle Paul for longer than an hour or so without recognizing that he was intensely committed to Jesus Christ? His actions didn't change when his friends were watching, when his enemies were watching, or even when no one was watching. Paul maintained his solid commitment to Jesus under any and all circumstances.

We need to discover what Paul knew—that when we learn to make Jesus our #1 commitment, all our other commitments will fall into place (friends, family, free time, school, jobs, and so forth). It's really easy to say or think that God is our top priority when actually we spend only a small fraction of our time involved with spiritual things.

Look over your list of completed sentences and search for indications of commitments that may be robbing Jesus of the top position. Then think through some ways you can begin to scale down on those commitments until your commitment to Jesus is once again first. You can receive a number of personal benefits from this exercise: an ability to see things from a new perspective, a calmness and order to your usually hectic life, and the knowledge that you will have His support during any crisis you might face. Total commitment to Jesus is the antidote to fear, boredom, confusion, loneliness, and dozens of other problems.

You may never face a series of legal trials for your faith as Paul had to. But your "trials" may be just as severe. And if you ever feel like giving up, just remember that you're a good friend of the Judge.

 **KEY VERSES**

"I have had God's help to this very day, and so I stand here and testify to small and great alike. I am saying nothing beyond what the prophets and Moses said would happen—that the Christ would suffer and, as the first to rise from the dead, would proclaim light to His own people and to the Gentiles" (Acts 26:22-23).

GUILTY AS SIN, BUT OFF SCOT-FREE

(Romans 1—5)

"Good evening, ladies and gentlemen, and welcome to 'The Righteousness Game'—the show where contestants have the opportunity to let the world know exactly how righteous they have been. I'm your host, Gooden Plenty. And you, our studio reading audience, will get to select the winner. So listen closely as each contestant presents his or her case. Contestant Number 1, tell us your name and then let us know: How righteous are you?"

"Thanks, Good. My name is Wanda Wonderful, and boy, am I righteous. You see, righteousness comes naturally for me. My husband is a pastor who has led 3,192 people to the Lord. My father was a pastor who led 1,813 people to the Lord. My grandfather and great-grandfather were both pastors, but they ministered in the days before people started keeping accurate statistics. I personally have a perfect attendance record in Sunday School that goes back to 1948. (I had to miss one Sunday then when I caught the black plague on top of a severe case of typhoid.) I fill in for our church organist on occasion, and I organize most of our church functions. What do I win?"

"Nothing, my dear," says Contestant Number 2. "What makes you think that righteousness is something that runs in your blood, or that you can inherit? My name is Les Best, and I know for a fact that righteousness is something you have to *study* for. I personally began at the age of 12 when I started street preaching. I went to a Christian high school, a Christian college, and earned a doctorate of righteousness from the finest Christian graduate school in the nation. I have written books and articles on how to be righteous (using myself as an example, of course). My three sons, Holy, Upright, and Howie are all following in my footsteps. I don't like to brag, of course, but all of them scored in the 700s on their Righteousness SATs."

At this point, Contestant Number 3 just has to interrupt. "Grow up, people. You can study all you want to or you can have a spotless background, but neither of those things will automatically make you righteous. You have to *work* at your righteousness. I know, and it strains my level of humility to refer to myself, Paula Perfect. I'm always on the go to get good deeds done. I lead a women's Bible study every week. I get up at 5:00 in the morning to go to prayer breakfasts. I give to missions and local civic groups. I even teach junior high Sunday School! They just don't come much more righteous than me!"

The host, Gooden Plenty, finally regains control of his show (just before the contestants start to fight for their right to be righteous). Turning to you, he says, "Which of our contestants do you think is the most righteous? And of course, we'll all want to know why." What will you tell him?

If you're tempted to say that none of these people seem all that righteous to you, you'll have to come up with your own definition (or illustration) of what *you* think righteousness is. Use the space below if you want to go that route.

 JOURNEY ONWARD

You may want to review your decision concerning righteousness after you finish this session. Righteousness was a key topic in the Book of Romans, Paul's letter to the church at Rome. As you go through this session, you will be quick to notice major differences between the Book of Acts and the Book of Romans. Acts was a historical narrative, action packed with fascinating events of the early church. Now, as we move into Romans, the tone will become more personal (though not as personal as some of Paul's other letters that we'll get to later). It's sort of like reading someone else's mail, though the things Paul wrote to the Romans apply to all Christians—then and now. The Book of Romans is filled with theological and doctrinal material, but don't let that fact scare you off. You'll also discover a lot of practical, applicable information that is just as helpful today as it ever was.

As Paul began his letter, what title did he give himself? (Romans 1:1)

What did Paul feel he was called to do? (1:1)

Did Paul think he was proclaiming a new truth? (1:2)

What did Paul teach about Jesus: that He was (1) a descendant of David, or (2) the Son of God? Explain your answer. (1:1-4)

A lot of people in the church at Rome were Gentile (non-Jewish) Christians. What did Paul want them to know as they read his letter? (1:5-6)

What good words did Paul have for the Roman Christians? (1:7-8)

What was Paul's wish as he wrote this letter? (1:9-15)

As Paul explained what he thought about the Gospel (the "Good News" about Jesus), he also revealed the source of righteousness. Where and how can someone obtain righteousness? (1:16-17)

Paul then contrasted righteousness with godlessness. How did he say that people become wicked and godless? (1:18-19)

How can people know about God, even if they may never have heard about Him? (1:20)

But when people try to ignore the signs of God that are around them, what often happens on a spiritual level? (1:21-23)

What happens on a physical level? (1:24-27)

What kind of lifestyle surrounds those who don't respond to God or His righteousness? (1:28-32)

Paul realized that problems could arise when he started contrasting righteousness with wickedness. He knew that a lot of people were likely to start comparing themselves to other people and think, "I'm more righteous than they are," or even, "Those guys are really rotten and I'm not all that bad." So what was the next thing Paul warned his readers of? (2:1-11)

Is a good knowledge of God's law all you need to be sure of your righteousness? Explain. (2:12-13)

Paul was shifting the focus of his message to his Jewish listeners for a while. He wanted them to know that just because they were Jews, they weren't automatically in God's favor. He pointed out that Gentiles who lived righteous lives honored God just as much as Jews (2:14-16). He then warned them against preaching about righteousness without living up to the standards that were being preached (2:17-23). What was happening because some Jews were demanding righteousness from others but not practicing it themselves? (2:24)

Paul then brought up the subject of circumcision—the physical mark of the Jewish people (the males, at least). What he had to say must have confused some of his Jewish readers. He spoke of physical circumcision in contrast to circumcision of the heart. Read Romans 2:25-29 and summarize what Paul was saying.

Yet Paul was in no way trying to degrade the Jews. (Remember that he was a devout Jew himself.) What positive things did Paul have to say about the Jews? (3:1-2)

God had made many promises to the Jewish people, and Paul raised a logical question: Since the Jews had been unfaithful to God, wouldn't their unfaithfulness nullify God's responsibility to be faithful to them? How did Paul answer his own question? (3:3-4)

Paul realized that some of the people might misinterpret what he was saying. He had boldly stated that God's faithfulness really stood out against the unfaithfulness of most people. So was Paul saying that it was actually a pretty good idea for us to disobey once in a while so God's faithfulness would come shining through? Explain (3:5-8).

According to Paul, who were more righteous— the Jews or the Gentiles? Explain (3:9-18).

What did Paul say was the purpose of the Jewish law? (3:19-20)

What is the source of true righteousness, and how can it be acquired? (3:21-24)

How did Jesus' death on the cross affect sins that had previously been committed? (3:25-26)

JUSTIFICATION
Why is it wrong to brag about what a good person you are? (3:27-31)

You may have noticed a word that Paul used frequently throughout this section. "All have sinned and fall short of the glory of God, and are *justified* freely by His grace through the redemption that came by Christ Jesus" (3:23-24); "A man is *justified* by faith apart from observing the law" (3:28); and "God . . . will *justify* the circumcised by faith and the uncircumcised through that same faith" (3:30). *Justification* is a big word for a big concept—yet it's not all that hard to understand.

When people come to grips with their sin and acknowledge that they can do nothing aside from putting their faith in Jesus to forgive those sins, then God can "justify" those people. First, because of Jesus' sacrificial death, God can declare the person "not guilty." But that's not all. He can go beyond that and declare the person "righteous." This righteousness is a gift from God (1:17) and is a result of His grace (3:24). (*Grace* refers to a gift that is unearned.) We did nothing to deserve God's forgiveness or His righteousness, but because of our faith in Jesus, we can receive both. And that is called *justification*.

Some people like to remember the definition of justification by thinking it is "just-as-if-I never sinned." Such a definition comes close to defining the end result of justification. But we should never forget that indeed we all *have* sinned, and part of justification is our conscious recognition and God's specific forgiveness of those sins.

When Paul started talking about being justified by faith rather than by obedience to God's law, he knew he might meet some resistance from the Jews. So he used their #1 forefather (Abraham) as an example. How did he say that Abraham was declared righteous? (4:1-8)

What was the connection between Abraham's righteousness and his circumcision? (4:9-12)

In what ways did Abraham's faith and righteousness benefit him? (4:13-21)

What are we supposed to learn from Abraham's example? (4:22-25)

In what ways will our own faith and righteousness benefit us? (5:1-2)

And knowing that we have been justified (forgiven and declared righteous), how can we learn to rejoice even during times of suffering? (5:3-5)

What is one of the most noteworthy things about Jesus' sacrifice for us? (5:6-8)

And because you have been justified in the past (when you became a Christian), what can you look forward to in the future? (5:9-11)

A NEW ADAM

Paul reminded his readers that their problem with sin had originally begun with one person—Adam (5:12-14). But just as one person had allowed sin to enter the world, another Person (Jesus) had eliminated the

fatal results of sin. As Paul compared Adam with Jesus, he noted several contrasts between sin and salvation. Read Romans 5:15-19 and list
as many of the differences as you can find.

What happened as sin began to spread? (5:20-21)

If you've been reading through this session and thinking that it's a little
more complicated or harder to read than past sessions have been, don't
worry too much. When you were younger, you might have had a fasci-
nation with any number of things. Take frogs, for instance. You may
have seen tadpoles hatch in your schoolroom or you may have just
watched frogs hopping around and having a good time. But when you
hit your first biology class and had to dissect one, you got quite a different perspective on frogs. You had to study their internal organs, observe their skeletal and circulatory systems, and eventually had to
learn a lot that you didn't necessarily *want* to know about frogs. But it
was important to learn because that lesson applied to lots of other
things.

The first part of the Book of Romans kind of dissects Christianity and
lets us see it from a different angle. We may prefer to assume that God
loves us and forgives us, and then just go about our lives. But we really
need to pause long enough to see *why* we believe a lot of things that we
usually take for granted.

Don't get discouraged if you don't understand everything right away.
Paul will touch on some of these same topics in later letters, and most
of these things will begin to make sense eventually. (To be truthful, you
can dwell on some of these issues a lifetime and never fully understand
them all.)

THE JOURNEY INWARD

One thing you *should* be able to understand with no trouble is the difference between righteousness and unrighteousness. You may not yet have familiarized yourself with all the technical aspects of justification, but you probably have a pretty good idea of what's right and what's wrong. So spend a few minutes evaluating your personal level of **righteousness.**

Paul provided us with a detailed, specific checklist of unrighteous actions and attitudes in Romans 1:29-31. He then went on to describe people who "know God's righteous decree" yet "continue to do these very things" (1:32). At first reading, we might not think the list applies to us at all. But could we possibly be guilty of willingly leading unrighteous lives? Let's find out.

Here is Paul's list broken down. Following each item on the list, mark the column that best describes your involvement in that particular element of unrighteousness.

Perhaps after completing your checklist you will discover a number of areas where, truthfully, you could stand some improvement. (If you don't find anything you're doing wrong on this list, you're certainly an exceptional model of the human species.) Your goal shouldn't necessarily be to reduce your list from eight offenses to three. Rather, your efforts should be spent in eliminating *all* these elements of unrighteousness from your life—whether you're guilty of eighteen, eight, or even only one.

The place to start is with prayer—first with an honest confession of the sins in your life, then with a request for the strength and courage to eliminate those sins, and finally with praise to the God who is able to forgive and declare you righteous.

As you saw in the introduction to this session, righteousness is not something that you can inherit, study for, or work to earn. It is a gift from God—a gift that originates only with a right relationship with Him.

	I would never be guilty of this!	I might act like this under extreme conditions.	Who knows? I might be like this.	I'm like this more often than I'd like to admit.	This is really me!
Wicked/evil					
Greedy					
Full of depravity (corrupt/ perverted)					
Envious					
Murderous					
Full of strife (always giving everyone a hard time)					
Deceitful					
Malicious (just plain mean)					
Gossipy					
Slanderous (speaking badly about others with harmful intent)					

	I would never be guilty of this!	Maybe under extreme conditions.	Who knows? I might be like this.	I'm like this more often than I'd like to admit.	This is really me!
God-hating					
Insolent (defiant in speech or actions)					
Arrogant (stuck-up)					
Boastful					
Inventor of new ways to do evil					
Disobedient to parents					
Senseless					
Faithless					
Heartless					
Ruthless					
Approving of other people who do evil					

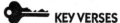 **KEY VERSES**

"I am not ashamed of the Gospel, because it is the power of God for the salvation of everyone who believes: first for the Jew, then for the Gentile. For in the Gospel a righteousness from God is revealed, a righteousness that is by faith from first to last, just as it is written: 'The righteous will live by faith'" (Romans 1:16-17).

SUPERNATURAL HONOR SOCIETY

(Romans 6—11)

Suppose you're on a plane ready to take off and this message comes over the intercom: "Good morning, ladies and gentlemen. This is your captain and I'd like to welcome you all on behalf of Random Air—the airline where you don't always get what you expect. We'll be taking off soon, but first I need to explain our seating arrangements. You see, 10 percent of our seating is in the first-class section, and we select those passengers at random. Yes, I realize that some of you paid three times as much for your ticket as others, but that doesn't matter. Today our first-class passengers will be those who, oh, I don't know, let's say those who are wearing high-topped tennis shoes."

As many of the young people (and a few of the stranger grandmothers) joyfully flock to the front of the plane for Caesar salads and Beef Wellington, the flight attendants would begin to serve the business people bologna sandwiches and peanuts. Needless to say, a lot of people would be less than satisfied—especially those who had paid a large price for a privilege they didn't receive.

Or suppose the principal of your school gets on the P.A. system one day and announces: "The faculty members have met and put together a list of 'special' people. The students on this list will be excused from school every Friday for the rest of the year. And at the end of the year these people will be sent on an all-expense paid field trip to Whimsy World, the nearby amusement park."

As the list is read (alphabetically), you hear many of your friends express their discontent when they don't hear their names. Some of the people with the highest grade-point averages are overlooked, as are several of the best athletes. Other popular people with good credentials stand openmouthed as they hear names of people they didn't even know existed. The "honor roll" includes troublemaking students who regularly threaten their teachers, campus bullies, "slow" students, and people that no one in their right minds would ever single out for special attention. All you can figure is that some standard was used for the selection of this list that you'll never be able to figure out.

By now you're probably thinking that these illustrations just aren't fair. And you're right. Air passengers who pay more *should* receive first-class treatment. Students who work hard *should* be recognized and rewarded. Yet as we saw in the last session, we must be careful that we don't apply these same expectations to righteousness. It is God who justifies us, and salvation is a free gift available to all. It's not limited to the richest, the most powerful, or the busiest people.

This session introduces another big, religious word. You struggled with the concept of justification in session 6. Now we move on to *sanctification*. The two words are closely related. After God justifies us (declares us righteous), He then sanctifies us. Simply put, we become set apart for better things. As non-Christians we are sinful, selfish, and worldly. But as new Christians who have just been declared righteous, we begin a transition of attitudes and actions that reflects our new priorities. So sanctification involves both a separation from sinful things and a setting apart to commit ourselves to the holy work of God. (You might want to consult a good Bible dictionary for a more complete definition.)

As we move forward in the Book of Romans, we'll learn more about this concept of being set apart. Paul doesn't actually use the word *sanctification* in this section, but later on you'll find the concept called by name.

 JOURNEY ONWARD

This part of Romans begins with a question that Paul has already hinted at a time or two (Romans 3:5-8). "If God is willing to heap forgiveness on us whenever we sin, should we keep sinning so God will keep forgiving?" How did Paul answer his own question? (6:1-2)

In what way are Christians set apart from the rest of the world? (6:3-4)

What did Paul say was one certain way to get out of being a slave? (6:5-7)

While dying may not sound attractive at first, there are several benefits of "dying" with Jesus. What are they? (6:8-14)

You may need to stretch your brain cells a little to understand what Paul was saying here, but it's not really too difficult. The thought is that Jesus died (physically) and rose again to free the world from the bondage of sin. We can also choose to "die" to sin (figuratively) after receiving Jesus' forgiveness. As sanctified (set apart) people who are "dead" (as far as our old, sinful natures are concerned), we are no longer under the control of sin and are free to live our lives for Christ instead.

Of course, our sanctification doesn't immediately make us sinless and perfect. But we should become more aware of the sins in our lives and consciously attempt to eliminate them. According to Paul, we should learn to respond to temptation the same way we would if we were dead. (And dead people don't sin very much.) Then with patience, practice, and discipline, we can train ourselves to remove much of the sin that may have previously controlled our lives.

Yet while we have been set free from the bondage of sin, we have become slaves in another sense. In what way are we slaves? (6:15-18)

What is the ultimate outcome of someone who never allows Jesus to free him (or her) from the bonds of sin? (6:19-22)

What makes it possible to avoid such an outcome? (6:23)

Paul then illustrated what he has been saying by referring to marriage. How was a woman legally released from her marriage vow? (7:1-3)

So how were the Jewish people released from the law (to the extent
that they could worship Jesus freely)? (7:4-6)

What purpose, then, did the law serve? (7:7-13)

Paul then described a personal struggle. What problem had he experienced in his spiritual life? (7:14-23)

What solution did Paul find for his spiritual problem? (7:24-25)

SPIRIT LIVING
What is the status of sinful people who put their trust in Jesus? (8:1-4)

What is one of the major differences between a sinful person and a renewed, spiritual person? (8:5-8)

Paul warned his readers that what he was saying should not be taken lightly. He emphasized that the life he was describing was possible only by the Holy Spirit's control of a person (8:9). He explained that we were to begin to put more of a focus on the spiritual aspects of our lives rather than the physical (8:10-11). And he made it clear that our choice in this matter is a life-or-death decision (8:12-14).

Yet in spite of all the weighty implications that Paul was describing, he also plainly stated why God desires that we make the right choice. When someone makes the decision to become led by the Holy Spirit, what kind of relationship does that person have with God? Be specific. (8:15-17)

[NOTE: *Abba* is an Aramaic word for father and indicates a very close relationship (like your use of the word *Daddy*).]

As you can tell, Paul wasn't afraid to deal with the harsh realities of things like sin and death, but his overall focus was positive. As you went through the Book of Acts, you saw that many times he had to suffer for what he believed. Here in Romans, he described how he felt about his suffering. What was Paul's attitude toward his previous sufferings? (8:18)

Paul wasn't the only one looking forward to seeing the power of God revealed. What else did Paul say was waiting for God to restore order? (8:19-22)

What other group should be waiting with hopeful anticipation? (8:23-25)

What role does the Holy Spirit play in this waiting process? (8:26-27)

What special benefit do God's people experience as they undergo problems and suffering? (8:28-29)

What does God hold back from His people? (8:30-34)

How much is Jesus committed to those who have put their trust in Him? (8:35-39)

It seems that as Paul wrote about the remarkable joys and privileges of being among God's people, his heart went out to his fellow Jews who refused to believe in Jesus as their Saviour. What did Paul say he might wish he could do if the Jewish people would only recognize the truth of the Gospel? (9:1-3)

HISTORY LESSON

Paul went on to remind his readers that the Jews had, throughout history, laid the groundwork for the coming of Jesus—through their covenants, the law, their temple worship, their genealogy, and so forth (9:4-5). But he also pointed out several examples where God had chosen to carry out His plans in a nontraditional manner. For instance, God's covenant with Abraham was carried out through Isaac (Sarah's child) instead of Ishmael (Hagar's child), who was born first (9:7-9). And Isaac's younger son, Jacob, was chosen over his older brother, Esau, to be the father of the Israelites (9:10-13).

Next, Paul pointed out that we shouldn't think God is unfair if He wants to do things in an unexpected manner. After all, nobody really deserves to receive what God gives us. Yet He has mercy on many of us while others harden themselves to what He has to offer. What illustration did Paul use to make his point clear? (9:19-21)

Paul then went back into the Old Testament Scriptures and pulled out quotations from Isaiah (quoted in Romans 9:27-29, 33) and Hosea (quoted in Romans 9:25-26). These passages reminded his readers that God had foreseen the inclusion of the Gentiles into His kingdom as well as the rejection of Jesus by many of the Jews. What was the big problem that many of the Jews had regarding righteousness? (9:30-32)

Why was the zeal of the Jews insufficient? (10:1-4)

What did Paul explain was necessary for salvation? (10:5-10)

Previously, circumcision had been the mark that differentiated a Jew from an "unclean" non-Jew. But after Jesus' death and resurrection, what was the spiritual significance of Jews and Gentiles? (10:11-13)

Paul again quoted Isaiah (52:7) as he reminds his readers of the secret to having beautiful feet. What is it? (Romans 10:14-15)

Yet many of the Jews who had heard the Good News hadn't responded. What were two bad attitudes among the Jewish people that prevented them from receiving the good things God had to offer them? (10:16-21, esp. v. 21)

But Paul wasn't saying that there was no hope for Israel. He emphasized that a number of them (a "remnant," or the "elect") had received the grace of God rather than continuing to try to be "worthy" of God's righteousness (11:1-10). Yet at the same time, what was taking place among the Gentiles? (11:11-12)

What illustration from nature did Paul use to illustrate how the Gentiles had become fruitful for God? (11:13-19)

Did Paul want the Gentiles to be boastful of their new status? Explain. (11:20-24)

What did Paul say Israel could expect in the future? (11:25-27)

Even though the Jews (as a whole) were being antagonistic toward the Gospel of Jesus, why didn't God just forget about them? (11:28-32)

Paul ended this portion of his writings with a short section of praise to God (11:33-36) before moving on to new things. In the next session you will see how Paul moved from this religious, doctrinal material into very practical applications of what it should mean in our day-to-day lives. So stay tuned. But for now, let's review some of the high points of what he brought out in this session.

 JOURNEY INWARD

It might make sense at this point to discuss the topic of sanctification at great length. But don't worry; we won't. Instead let's consider another topic that also pertains to being "set apart." For a few moments, turn your attention to the subject of **cliques.**

A clique is defined as "a narrow exclusive circle or group of persons, especially one held together by a presumed identity of interests, views, or purposes." We don't usually go around saying, "I belong to a clique." Instead, we refer to "the group," "the gang," or "my close circle of friends." And while some of our groups may be innocent enough, many of them exclude certain people and thereby qualify as cliques.

In the space below, list all the formal organizations to which you belong (at school and otherwise). Include sports teams, honor societies, music and drama clubs, and so forth.

Now think about all the informal groups you participate in—the people you hang around with at school, your lunchroom crowd, the group you play tennis with every week, etc. (Even if these are all the same people, list the different places you all get together.)

Now go back through your two lists and mark through any of the groups you belong to that are exclusive in any way—even if there's a good reason. For instance, the Boy Scouts are a fine organization, but they exclude girls. Your honor societies are great, but they exclude people with low grade-point averages. And even your informal groups may try to avoid certain people. So mark off every item on your lists that isn't completely open to everyone. Do your crossing off before you continue.

If you're like most people, you probably listed several different groups of which you are a member. But you probably had to mark off most of the groups as being exclusive in one way or another. That's why most of them were started in the first place—to single out certain kinds of people. And the informal groups we form just naturally follow the same pattern. We unite with people we like and tend to keep out people we don't.

Yet as Christians we belong to the only "set apart" group that really matters. God has made us righteous and has set us apart from the rest of the world to do good work for Him. We're supposed to treat everyone equally. We're instructed to love everyone—friend and enemy alike. And membership in God's sanctified group of people should take precedence over any of our other bonds. God set us apart so we could help recruit other people. Yes, we're special to God, but so is everyone else. We should do all we can do to make sure our Christian "club" is as nonexclusive as we can make it (by bringing in other people as often as possible).

We should try to get rid of senseless habits and traditions that needlessly set us apart from other people for no good reason. And we must beware that even our church groups don't turn into "safe" places for us where "outsiders" feel unwelcome. The Jews had become little more than a clique that excluded everyone who might challenge their religious tradition or cause them discomfort. And Paul had to deal harshly with them as he turned his attention to the Gentiles who were ready to respond to the Gospel of Jesus Christ.

If we are to be set apart, let's be set apart for the right reason. Let's be set apart for God, continually reaching out to help others be set apart as well. And let's forget about trying so hard to set ourselves apart only to boast and make other people hurt or jealous. Ours should always be the beautiful feet that take the Good News of Jesus to others.

 **KEY VERSES**

"The Spirit Himself testifies with our spirit that we are God's children. Now if we are children, then we are heirs—heirs of God and co-heirs with Christ, if indeed we share in His sufferings in order that we may also share in His glory" (Romans 8:16-17).

GET BACK ON THAT ALTAR!

(Romans 12—16)

Once upon a time two ambassadors traveled a long distance to visit a powerful king. They had heard that an alliance with this king would provide their countries great benefits. The reputation of this king's wealth and might was known far and wide.

As the ambassadors rode across the drawbridge that spanned the vast moat, they soon came upon a stableboy. The first ambassador spoke authoritatively: "Quick, boy, take care of our horses. We have important business to attend to with your king!" The stableboy replied with a snappy "Yes, sir" as he saw to their mounts.

As they approached the castle, the first ambassador leaned toward the other and whispered, "You have to show these people their place. By doing so, their king will get word that we too are men to be reckoned with." The second ambassador wasn't by nature a harsh person, but he agreed to follow the lead of his companion.

The two men entered the castle and were greeted by a maid. She explained that the king had prepared a great feast in honor of the two special guests. Her demeanor was pleasant and her speech was filled with "Begging your pardons, sirs." Yet when she showed the ambassadors their rooms, both said, "Goodness no; this will not do." And they had her prepare larger, more elegant accommodations.

While strolling around the castle before dinner, the ambassadors saw a workman attempting to unearth a large stump from the ground. While his mule pulled with all its might, the man used a large branch as a lever to pry the stump up. When the ambassadors saw the man struggling, one immediately started to help him. But the first one held him back and said, "Maintain your dignity, by all means." Then the first ambassador began to ridicule the workman with phrases such as: "You're as weak as a washerwoman;" "Why don't you and the mule trade places, because he looks like the smart one;" and others too vulgar to tell in this story.

After several minutes of verbal abuse, the workman walked over to the ambassadors. And what a contrast they made—they with their fine silk clothes, and he all sweaty, covered with dirt, and smelling of the stables. The workman said simply, "With your fair skin and soft hands, what makes you such an authority on real work?"

But instead of answering him, the first ambassador responded with a vicious SLAP that caused the workman to stagger backward. "Your king will hear of this insult tonight, you impudent lowlife," shouted the ambassador as his friend looked on with a shocked expression. The workman only sighed softly and said, "I'm sure he will." Then he walked away.

An hour later the two ambassadors were seated in the places of honor at the banquet table. They heard trumpets blow and a voice that said, "Please rise for the royal family." And as the ambassadors turned toward the entrance, their fair skin turned even whiter. For as they watched, in walked the stableboy, the maid, and the workman. But how different they looked! Each was wearing what looked like precious gems that had somehow been spun into clothing (and which made the ambassadors' silk clothing seem bland in comparison). They walked with pride and confidence, and a crown was on each one's head. They took their seats—one directly across from the ambassadors and one on either side.

The "workman" spoke first. "I am the king of this territory and these are my children. In fact, everyone in this kingdom is an adopted child with all the rights due a prince or princess."

The first ambassador finally gathered his wits enough to reply. "If you are all royalty, why did you try to trick us by acting like mere servants?"

The maid/princess answered. "We surely did not try to trick you, sir. You see, everyone in this kingdom is committed to the life of a servant. We are truly royalty, but we serve willingly."

"Yes," added the workman/king, "and anyone who would ally themselves with us must adopt our practices."

The first ambassador stood up defiantly. "Forget it. Speaking for my people, I can tell you that we would never consider your customs. It makes you weak and common." Then he stormed out of the room to return home.

The king turned to the other ambassador and asked softly, "How about you, my son?"

The man (who was at least as old as the king and could hardly believe he would be considered as a son) could hardly hold back his tears. His voice cracked as he answered, "Sir, I would stay here longer and learn your ways."

"Good," said the king. "We start tomorrow." With a gesture from the king the stableboy/prince handed a package to the ambassador. The king explained, "Here is your royal robe, your crown, your workboots, and ointment for the blisters that you will surely have by this time tomorrow. But perhaps with your help, I can finish removing that stump."

Then they all sat down to eat, and the ambassador had never felt so much at home.

 JOURNEY ONWARD

In the last session you learned that Christians are God's children and heirs (Romans 8:15-17). We are entitled to what is His. But there was one condition—we must share in His suffering in order to share in His glory (v. 17). This session will help explain just how we are to do so.

Since God has been so merciful to us, what did Paul urge us to do for God? (12:1)

▌

Paul's suggestion is a strange one. Sacrifices were supposed to die. But then, you should also recall that we are supposed to be "dead" to our old sinful natures and alive to serving God (6:11). So instead of being a one-time-only sacrifice and then dying, we can remain alive to live sacrificially again and again.

Someone has jokingly pointed out that the big trouble with a living sacrifice is that it can keep crawling off the altar. How does Paul tell us we can faithfully respond to God's will? (12:2)

▌

What is one of the common problems that prevents people from acting sacrificially? (12:3)

Paul here used an illustration that he repeated in other letters. How did he illustrate the need for everyone to use his or her own spiritual gifts for the good of the church as a whole? (12:4-8)

Paul emphasized that love must be sincere (12:9). He also outlined a number of things to do (or not to do) that demonstrate sincere love. Read Romans 12:9-21 and list the things that you should and shouldn't do. (Write small. His list is extensive.)

THINGS YOU SHOULD DO	THINGS YOU SHOULDN'T DO

Paul's reference to heaping burning coals on your enemy's head is a quote from Proverbs 25:21-22. There is discussion about exactly what this phrase means. One common interpretation is that it was somewhat like our saying that we will "kill someone with kindness." In other words, goodness tends to win people over better than force or punishment.

Then Paul seemed to shift his focus from how to get along with our peers to how to get along with the people in authority over us. What attitude should we have toward our authority figures and why? (13:1)

How does God feel about people who rebel against authority? (13:2)

How do human leaders feel about people who rebel against authority? (13:3)

When we realize that our leaders are actually servants of God (whether they realize it or not), we should feel compelled to submit to them. If we're not afraid of what they might do if we disobey, why should we obey them anyway? (13:5)

Paul didn't want his readers to stop with submission in tangible ways (through taxes, revenue money, etc.). How did he instruct us to show our loyalty through intangible ways as well? (13:6-7)

Paul also told us to pay off all our debts except for one that can never really be declared "Paid in Full." What is that single permissible debt? (13:8)

How can you summarize the Ten Commandments with a single statement? (13:9-10)

Paul explained that we're "playing against the clock," so to speak. He knew that Jesus has promised to return, and that we shouldn't waste time "sleeping" (doing things that God doesn't want us to do). Specifically, what does Paul instruct his readers to do? (13:11-14)

WEAKER BROTHERS

So according to Paul, we're supposed to become living sacrifices by loving both friends and enemies, and by submitting to those in authority. But how about those people who are somewhat "beneath" us spiritually? How should we treat people whose faith hasn't quite developed to our own high standard? (14:1)

What was one issue that not all the Roman Christians agreed on? (14:2-4)

What was another issue that sparked disagreement? (14:5-6)

What do we need to understand that will help us quit complaining about the weaknesses of other people? (14:7-8)

Why is it so wrong to judge others? (14:9-12)

Paul practiced what he preached. He felt it improper to place what he called a "stumbling block" in front of a weaker brother who might get tripped up on it. What example of a potential stumbling block did Paul draw from his own experience to use as an illustration? (14:13-18)

One option we have is to insist on practicing our Christian freedom with all of its "rights" and "privileges"—no matter what the effect is on other people. But what is a more preferable option? (14:19-23)

What is the responsibility of people who have strong faith? (15:2)

Why should they carry out their responsibility? (15:3-4)

What was Paul's wish for his readers? (15:5-6)

Paul had good reasons for asking his readers to accept one another. When the church at Rome first read his letter, the big tension was between the Jewish Christians and the Gentile Christians. Centuries of history had kept the Jews and non-Jews at odds with each other, but Jesus' death was going to bring them together (15:7-13). The shift in thinking was bound to cause some problems, and Paul's letter kept reminding the Roman Christians to work hard at getting along.

We mustn't think, however, that Paul's instructions are outdated. Christians today are just as divided as ever. Much conflict, bitterness, and even hatred have taken place in the guise of holding fast to our religion (as opposed to *their* religion). Can you think of any "religious" conflicts you've witnessed lately that would have been avoided if the people involved had been a little more tolerant?

How did Paul feel about his readers? (15:14-16)

Paul hadn't yet visited the church in Rome. Why not? (15:17-22)

What were Paul's plans for the future? (15:23-29)

What did Paul want from the readers of his letter? (15:30-33)

Paul concluded his letter by sending greetings *to* the individuals he knew personally in Rome (16:1-16) and *from* the people who were with him (16:21-23). As a note of interest, Romans 16:22 indicates that Paul probably dictated this letter to a secretary. Yet even as Paul was wrapping up his message, he left one more word of warning tucked away among the greetings. What thought did he leave with his readers? (16:17-20)

Was Paul worried about the Christians at Rome? Explain (16:25-27).

On that note Paul ended his letter to the Christians at Rome. And we move on to see how this section of Romans applies to us.

 **JOURNEY INWARD**

You probably noticed that chapters 12–16 of Romans have a lot more personal application than the first eleven chapters. This latter section contains a lot of specific instructions, but they are all included under one general command. And it is that command that we want to examine before we move on. So let's figure out some common-sense ways for **becoming a living sacrifice.**

If you've been through the Old Testament BibleLog books, you may remember a little about the requirements for a sacrifice. The animal had to be a firstborn that was perfect. Weak, sick, scrawny animals were rejected. Everyone who came into contact with the sacrifice had to be cleansed—the priest, the animal handlers, and even the person who "took out the trash" that was left behind after the offering had been made. (See Leviticus 16 for a detailed description.) No hint of imperfection could be allowed. Yet once the animal was sacrificed, it was dead and didn't have to worry anymore. But what do you think is entailed by being a *living* sacrifice?

It would be nice if we could list a specific number of actions to take in order to become a productive living sacrifice. But no number of actions will get the job done. If you're observant, you probably noticed that the first step in becoming a living sacrifice is an *inner* action—a renewing of your mind that transforms you (Romans 12:2). Only after you experience the inner change will you be able consistently to produce sacrificial actions.

With these thoughts in mind, try to imagine yourself as a truly committed living sacrifice to the glory of God. How do you think you would respond in each of the following situations that were described by Paul?

(1) SHOWING LOVE TO OTHERS
Review your list of do's and don'ts on page 98. It might seem impossible to obey the instructions on that list consistently . But if you cared only about honoring God rather than satisfying your own desires, do you think anything on the list would be too unreasonable? Explain.

(2) SUBMISSION TO AUTHORITIES
If you were committed to being a living sacrifice, how would your relationships with authority figures change? (Think of parents, teachers, coaches, principals, police, pastors, and so forth.) Be specific.

(3) RELATING TO "WEAKER" CHRISTIANS
Can you think of any issues that divide you from other Christians (per-

haps drinking, dancing, church traditions, etc.)? Or can you think of any "stumbling blocks" that prevent you (or that you use to prevent others) from feeling comfortable with your Christianity? If so, list them below and explain how sacrificial living might remove some of those obstacles.

Frankly, it's pretty easy to become a Christian and then quickly get caught up in the rules, habits, traditions, and other trappings. These things aren't usually bad in themselves, but they can hinder spontaneity and the challenge of creatively maturing each day into a more effective living sacrifice. Can you think of any changes you might need to make in your actions or attitudes before you can be a good living sacrifice? If so, list them below.

Finally, ask God to help you learn to go through each day as a living sacrifice (beginning with the renewal of any improper thought patterns). And try not to miss future opportunities to show love to others, willingly submit to authorities, or give up your "rights" in order to help a weaker Christian. It's not easy to stay on the altar, but with a renewed mind that's in tune with God's will, it *can* be done.

🔑 KEY VERSE

"I urge you, brothers, in view of God's mercy, to offer your bodies as living sacrifices, holy and pleasing to God—this is your spiritual act of worship" (Romans 12:1).

OH, GROW UP!

(1 Corinthians 1—4)

It's an average morning in your household. Mom and Dad ate breakfast earlier on their way to work. Little brother is fixing instant oatmeal in the microwave. You decide to go with "the usual," so you toddle over to the refrigerator and get a bottle of milk—one with a fresh nipple on the bottle. Then you peruse the pantry to see what else you want. Strained peas? No, you had them yesterday. You take a pass on the mashed carrots too, finally selecting the creamed asparagus. Yummy!

After breakfast you get yourself dressed—fresh diapers, of course, and your cute yellow jumpsuit with the moo-moo cows on it. Little brother has to help you tie your shoes again. You still don't have those knots figured out.

Then you toss your books and homework into your book satchel and head for the door. (You hope your teacher will explain who this "Spot" person is who seems to run around with Dick and Jane so much.) And since the big hand is already on the eight, you know you have to hurry. So you hop on your tricycle and pedal just as hard as you can.

You don't go to the same school that most of the people your age do. They take strange-sounding subjects like algebra, civics, chemistry, and social studies. Your classes are simpler: arithmetic, reading, and your favorite—recess.

All right, all right. Maybe this *isn't* an average morning at your house. It's kind of ridiculous to imagine that someone your age with normal mental abilities has refused to grow up. Growth is natural and it provides variety in life. As you mature, you experience new sensations— new foods, sights, friends, activities, skills, responsibilities, accomplishments, and so forth. The alternative to growth is stagnation, which is almost always accompanied by boredom. Life can get pretty monotonous if you never attempt anything new or different.

The same principle holds true on a spiritual level. Becoming a Christian should be only the first step in a long growing process. (Jesus' phrase "born again" [John 3:3] is a good description.) Someone who becomes a Christian but refuses to mature as a Christian is about as attractive as an adult wearing diapers and drinking from a baby bottle.

 JOURNEY ONWARD

This session takes us into 1 Corinthians, and Paul is going to have some straightforward words about maturing as a Christian. His letter is addressed to the church in Corinth (Greece), and boy, did they have problems! First Corinthians is a more "gritty" letter than Romans. Paul's letter to Rome was pretty heavy and intellectual. But his first letter to the Corinthians is clear and practical. The people in Corinth were struggling with a lot of the same problems that we have, and Paul's advice is still helpful as we are hassled with sexual temptation, fear of death, jealousy, and the struggle for spiritual maturity. So leave your diapers and baby food behind, and let's do some growing up.

Paul had begun the Book of Romans by calling himself a "servant" of Christ Jesus. What did he call himself as he began 1 Corinthians? (1:1)

When you compare the two words, what does it suggest Paul felt was the role of an apostle?

As Paul greeted the church, he reminded them that they are "sanctified in Christ Jesus and called to be holy" (1:2). If you remember what you learned about sanctification in session 7, you'll recognize that Paul was encouraging the Corinthian Christians to be "set apart" from the rest of the world. (You'll soon find out that they weren't.) Who else did Paul address in his salutation? (1:2)

Judging from Paul's opening greeting, we can expect the material in 1 Corinthians to be just as applicable to us as it was to the Christians in Corinth. He confronted them (and us) about several areas where their wrongdoing needed to be corrected and eliminated. Yet he didn't tear into them right away. He opened tactfully (and honestly) by noting some positive things he had observed about the Corinthian church. What noteworthy accomplishments did Paul point out concerning the Corinthians? (1:4-9)

But then Paul moved right into his purpose for writing. What was his appeal to them? (1:10)

What was one of the big problems in the church at Corinth? (1:11-12)

Paul dealt more completely with this problem in 1 Corinthians 3, but he made a couple of statements at this point. He tried not to take much credit for the work he had done for Jesus. What did Paul know would happen if people got caught up in his "wise" words? (1:13-17)

Paul didn't want people to be won over to the Gospel because of his own persuasive abilities as a speaker. (What if an even more persuasive person came along promoting a different religion?) Paul wanted people to respond to the sacrificial death of Jesus on their behalf. Yet Paul clearly understood that people would respond to the Gospel message with drastically different opinions. What opinions did Paul describe? (1:18-24)

- The opinion of nonbelieving Jews—

- The opinion of nonbeliving Gentiles—

- The opinion of believing Jews and Gentiles—

How does our wisdom stack up to God's wisdom? (1:25)

Who does God often choose to work through? Why? (1:26-29)

When is boasting permissible? (1:30-31)

From your readings in the Book of Acts, you may have an image of Paul as someone who was *always* bold, courageous, and strong. But how did he describe his first contact with the Corinthians? (2:1-5)

What kind of people can understand the wisdom of the Gospel? (2:6)

Why doesn't everyone understand it? (2:7-10)

What is the role of the Holy Spirit in our understanding? (2:11-15)

At this point, Paul asked a question first asked by Isaiah: "Who has known the mind of the Lord?" (1 Corinthians 2:16; Isaiah 40:13) Paul was able to respond to this question that Isaiah had left unanswered. What was available for Paul that hadn't been accessible to Isaiah? (1 Corinthians 2:16)

FAT BABIES
Then Paul got a little more personal with the Corinthian Christians. After explaining that only spiritual people could understand the Gospel,

he said something to the effect of, "Oh, by the way, you people aren't spiritual" (3:1). How did Paul illustrate the fact that the Corinthians were still "mere infants" in their spiritual development? (3:2)

What made it so easy for Paul to tell that the Corinthians were immature Christians? (3:3-4)

Paul then responded to the argument that he had referred to earlier (1:12). Apparently the people in the Corinthian church were taking sides over whom they wanted to follow. Some were really behind Paul. Some liked Peter better. Others had decided that Apollos was their man. (You may remember Apollos from Acts 18:24-28). And, of course, some of the Corinthians were saying, "Well, *we* follow Jesus. Nyah, nyah, nyah!" Paul tried to clarify the confusion over everyone's role in the spread of the Gospel. How did he explain it? (3:5-9)

Paul compared himself to a builder. He explained that when he told the Corinthians about Jesus, it was as if he had laid the foundation of a house for each person who believed. And from that point, it was up to the person to build on the foundation he or she had been provided. Some people might build on their foundations with high-quality work, symbolized by gold, silver, and precious gems. Others might not try so hard to build on their foundations, and their work might be the quality of wood, hay, or straw. Why is it important to work hard and build well on the foundation that has been provided us? (3:10-15)

The point the Corinthians were missing was that the church body composed God's temple and anything that tore apart that temple would be held against them (3:16-17). Rallying behind different leaders was senseless, because Peter, Paul, and Apollos all belonged to the same body of believers. So what advice did Paul give on this matter? (3:18-23)

What alternative did Paul suggest to the Corinthians, rather than holding up spiritual leaders as personal heroes? (4:1)

Paul knew it was important for the church members to have a responsible attitude toward its leaders. But he also knew that the leaders had a responsibility as well. What was the requirement for those who had authority in the church? (4:2)

What were the right and wrong ways Paul listed for an individual to evaluate his or her own effectiveness as a Christian? (4:3-4)

What did Paul tell those people who might want to make premature judgments concerning their leaders? (4:5)

Paul knew that the Corinthians' problem went beyond their division concerning whom they wanted to follow. Yet instead of pointing an accusing finger at guilty parties, he had used himself and Apollos as an example of how two people could "compete" in a sense, and still display humility. What did Paul identify as the general problem of the Corinthian church? (4:6)

∎

The Corinthians had been focusing on the differences between one person and another, only to cause divisions among themselves. Now Paul asked them a couple of simple questions to challenge their thinking. What questions did Paul ask them? (4:7)

∎

Then he got a little sarcastic. (As you continue through the letters of Paul, you'll see that he got that way from time to time.) To paraphrase his comments, Paul said, "You people have everything you want, don't you? You're so rich! Why, you guys are kings! And I suppose we apostles didn't have a thing to do with it." Then Paul got serious for a moment and said he wished the Corinthians *had* become kings, so the apostles could share in their glory.

But in reality, apostles were nowhere close to "king" status. How did Paul describe the "honored" position of an apostle? (4:9-13—And note the additional sarcasm in v. 10.)

∎

Based on Paul's description, how well do you think you would perform the duties of an apostle? Explain.

∎

TOUGH LOVE

Paul might sound like he was trying to embarrass the Corinthian Christians or put them to shame. He admitted as much in other places, but that wasn't his intention here. Why was he so blunt with them? (4:14)

What kind of bond did Paul feel like he had with the Corinthians? (4:15)

What did Paul urge the Corinthians to do? (4:16)

What did Paul do to help the Corinthians? (4:17)

Why had some of the Corinthians been getting so sassy? (4:18)

What was Paul going to do to take care of the problem? (4:19)

What options did Paul leave with the Corinthians? (4:20-21)

In the next session you'll find out that the church at Corinth had problems even more serious than the ones Paul has addressed so far. But for now, let's evaluate and apply what we've seen to this point.

JOURNEY INWARD

It shouldn't have taken a great apostle to tell the Corinthians that their attitudes were way out of line. Anyone with open eyes and a little common sense could quickly figure out that the people in that church had some serious growing up to do. Similarly, it shouldn't take your pastor, youth worker, parents, or teachers to tell *you* how to shape up your own spiritual life. You should be able to analyze your thoughts, attitudes, habits, and actions to see if change is needed. And if you're aware of problem areas but just haven't gotten around to correcting them, perhaps you have the same root problem as the Corinthians. Maybe you need to consider the matter of **maturity** in your own Christian life.

If you haven't fully matured in certain areas of your Christian life, you first need to recognize the specific areas where you most need to grow. (For example, the Corinthians weren't ready for "solid" teaching because of their level of worldliness, so Paul could only give them "milk" [3:1-2].)

So for each of the categories in the chart, mark the level of growth that would most accurately reflect your current degree of maturity. Use the following key to help in your evaluation.

- ITTY BITTY BABY—So naive that you're unaware of your need for growth.
- TODDLER—Still totally dependent on others, yet willing to learn in small doses.
- YOUNGSTER—Beginning to do things for yourself, but somewhat self-centered.
- YOUNG TEEN—You have a knowledge of the "basics," yet are developing a certain degree of rebellion toward authority.
- TEENAGER—You're dealing with lots of problems, but choosing to mature in this area because you *want* to.
- ADULT—Still growing (most of the time) in spite of problems and obstacles.
- MATURE ADULT—Nothing can stop you from growing in this area. No way!

CATEGORIES	ITTY BITTY BABY	TODDLER	YOUNGSTER	YOUNG TEEN	TEENAGER	ADULT	MATURE ADULT
Knowledge of Scripture							
Regular, sincere prayer							
Respect for church leaders							
Equal treatment of others							
Ability to get along with others							
Treatment of family members							
Church attendance							
General behavior							
Good attitudes							
Clean thoughts							

Don't be too concerned if you rated yourself lower than you'd like in several categories. Christian maturity should be a lifelong process, and at this point in your life you should be in the early stages. At the same time, it's important that you now take the first steps (even if they're only baby steps) toward maturity. If you cease to grow while you're young, it's often very hard to start again later in life. To stunt your spiritual growth now can have severe consequences.

One other thing should be noted. Don't look for drastic results overnight. Spiritual maturity usually takes place gradually. When you're a little kid and your parents stand you against the wall on your birthday to see how much you've grown, you rarely see any two-foot jumps. But by growing a few inches each year, you eventually make it to adulthood. Your spiritual growth is likely to follow the same pattern. But the sooner you start, the more mature you'll be by this time next year.

 **KEY VERSE**

"The wisdom of the cross is foolishness to those who are perishing, but to us who are being saved it is the power of God" (1 Corinthians 1:18).

A SEXUALLY SUGGESTIVE MESSAGE

(1 Corinthians 5—7)

On a weekend camping trip, you get a site near Jim and Brad. They don't know you're there, because they're too busy staying up late, enjoying the stars, and talking about the deep mysteries of life (mostly girls). You don't really like to eavesdrop, but you just can't help it.

JIM: Don't you think there are a lot of dumb rules we have to follow just because adults don't want us to do certain things?

BRAD: Like what?

JIM: Oh, lots of things. Drugs, for instance. You know I don't smoke anything or do cocaine. But if I wanted to, what's the big deal? I mean, it's *my* body. Right? So why shouldn't I be free to decide what I want to do?

BRAD: And if you get addicted, or overdose and die, you don't think it would affect your parents? Or your grandparents? Or your little sister? Or *me?*

JIM: OK. Maybe you're right about drugs. What about sex?

BRAD: No thanks. I'm already dating someone.

JIM: Very funny, you weirdo. You know what I mean! What if Janie and I both agree that we want to have sex? If it's a mutual decision, there's no way either one of us gets hurt, right?

BRAD: I'm not so sure. You guys have been dating a long time and seem perfect for each other. But I just don't think two people can have sex without it drastically affecting their relationship. I've seen it break up a lot of couples already. In fact, of all the "serious" couples I've known, I don't know of any who got sexually involved who are still together.

JIM: But it seems like a natural next step for a relationship like ours.

BRAD: Don't you think everyone else thought so too? Suppose you and Janie decided to go all the way. What then? Are you ready to get married if she gets pregnant, or when you decide that's the only way your relationship can grow from that point? How will that influence your plans for college? And what if you do eventually break up? After having sex with one person, I'm not sure that I could ever get a serious relationship going with someone else—at least, not without a lot of guilt.

JIM: Yeah, yeah. You make a lot of sense now. But when Janie and I are alone together, staring at the full moon, we sometimes care a little more about romance than logic—believe it or not.

BRAD: Don't get smart with me, pal. I'm not arguing against romance. But I don't think you have to throw logic out the window when you fall in love. In fact, without a little common sense, your romance might not last very long.

At this point in their conversation, a stray molecule of pollen floats into your nose and forces you to sneeze loudly. Brad and Jim both whirl and look at you, somewhat sheepishly. But then Jim says, "Hey, this looks like a wise and friendly individual. Let's see what this intelligent person has to say about sex."

How would you comment on Jim's and Brad's observations? As you express your opinions, be sure to provide the reasons that you believe the way you do.

JOURNEY ONWARD

Many people go through a phase when they feel no obligation to anyone but themselves. During this phase, some people start drinking themselves silly every weekend. Others experiment with all kinds of drugs. Some just develop bad attitudes: "Leave me alone. I didn't *ask* to be born, you know!" And for a while, those people really think that nobody else in the world should be affected by their lives.

Most people grow out of that mind-set eventually, at least to some degree. But many of the people in the Corinthian church were still of the opinion that they should be able to do just about anything they wanted to do. And their misguided thinking was causing some serious problems.

You should remember from the last session that Paul had already confronted the Corinthian Christians concerning their lack of spiritual maturity. But in this session you will quickly discover that their spiritual immaturity had led to some other serious problems of a more earthy nature.

As usual, Paul was straightforward in his approach to the problem. What was the big offense in the Corinthian church? (1 Corinthians 5:1)

Paul was quick to point out that the Corinthian Christians were guilty of something that even non-Christians found horrendous. The use of the phrase "father's wife" may suggest that the woman in question was the man's stepmother rather than his flesh-and-blood mother. Even so, the relationship was clearly a sinful one. How did the Corinthians feel about this terrible sin in their midst? (5:2)

This attitude is probably similar to the one that Paul warned the Romans about—that the more we sin, the more God can forgive us (Romans 6:1-2). And from that attitude came the mistaken assumption that Christians were free to do just about anything they wanted to. That was what Christian liberty was all about, right? Paul answered with an emphatic, "Wrong!"

What did Paul instruct the church to do? (1 Corinthians 5:2-5)

What was the purpose of this disciplinary action? (5:5)

It may be easy to misinterpret Paul's intention. In regard to the man, Paul told them to have him "put out of your fellowship" and "hand this man over to Satan." In essence, Paul was saying that if the man was going to live *as* a heathen, let him live *with* the heathens (outside the church, in Satan's domain). Then if the guy had any sensitivity to the Holy Spirit, he would soon miss the fellowship with the rest of the church body. Eventually he would be ready to repent and be restored again into fellowship. But if the church didn't take action to remove him from their midst, it would seem as if God approved of the man's perverted relationship.

ONE BAD APPLE
As you can see, Paul didn't stop after dealing with the specific sin of the one person. He moved right into the attitude of the church as a whole.

What illustration did he use to demonstrate the effects of "a little" sin? (5:6-8—If you don't understand his reference to the Passover lamb and unleavened bread, review Exodus 12:1-13.)

In spite of Paul's harsh words concerning sexual immorality, he didn't limit his lecture to that area of sin. What other sins did he put on the same level with sexual sin? (1 Corinthian 5:9-11)

How should we relate to people who call themselves Christians yet are willingly entrenched in the sins that Paul listed? (5:11)

Paul suggests that our tendency as Christians is to pass judgment on non-Christians. What did he think about that tendency? Why? (5:12-13)

Most people know what Christians *say* they believe. But if our actions don't match our words, we do God's kingdom a lot more harm than good. And even if *you* are living out everything you believe in, a close friendship with someone who is "faking" his Christianity can cause others to suspect you as well. Your friendship could very possibly interfere with someone's being attracted to the Gospel of Christ.

If we begin to live as if the rest of the world is watching us, what's another big problem area we'll have to avoid? Why? (6:1-6)

How did Paul suggest this problem could be avoided? (6:4)

But then he provided an even better solution. What was it? (6:7-8)

Paul again reminded his readers that sexual immorality and the other sins he had already mentioned (5:9-11) cannot be part of the Christian lifestyle. He got very explicit about sexual sin at this point. What specific offenses did he include? (6:9-10)

He quickly acknowledged that these sins might have been included in the past of some of the Corinthian believers, but what had changed about those people? (6:11)

PERMISSION GRANTED?
Apparently some of the Corinthian Christians had the attitude that "everything is permissible for me," because Paul echoed that phrase more than once (6:12, and later in 10:23). After Paul mimicked that quotation, how did he modify it so the Corinthians couldn't justify doing anything they felt like doing? (6:12-14)

Paul probably anticipated that some of the stubborn Corinthians would argue, "It's my body and I'm not really hurting anyone, so what's the big deal?" Paul didn't agree that our bodies are ours to do with as we please. Why did he say we should be so careful not to "unite" with ungodly influences? (6:15-17)

How much should we be willing to tolerate sexual immorality? (6:18)

What reasons did Paul give to explain why we don't have the right to do whatever we want to do with our bodies? (6:19-20)

Paul chose to "honor God" as a single person. He wasn't married. He wasn't even interested in *thinking* about getting married. Yet he wasn't opposed to the institution of marriage. What was his advice? (7:1-2)

How important is sex within a marriage relationship? (7:3-7)

What guidelines did Paul give to unmarried Christians? (7:8-9)

What guidelines did Paul give to married Christians? (7:10-11)

What about Christians married to non-Christians? (7:12-16)

As Paul went through God's guidelines in all these areas, what did he say was the most important thing to keep in mind at all times? (7:17-19)

Some of the early Christians were slaves. Yet Paul kept talking about the freedom that could be gained through Christianity. What comfort did Paul have for the slaves who would be hearing his words? (7:20-24)

After his brief time-out to address the church on matters of status (circumcision, slavery, etc.), Paul turned his attention back to sexual guidelines for the misguided Corinthian church. He addressed the unmarried people and explained that he had no direct message from God telling them to either definitely get married or definitely stay single. What was Paul's opinion on the matter? Why? (7:25-28)

What can a single person do that a married person can't? (7:29-35)

Even though Paul was recommending that people stay single if possible, do you think he was saying that the single life was for everyone? Explain your answer (7:36-40).

What is your personal opinion? Do you think singleness is preferable to marriage? Do you think marriage is preferable? Or does it matter?

While Paul openly admitted whenever he was sharing his opinion rather than passing along a direct message from God, do you think the Corinthians would receive his opinion casually? Explain (7:40).

One point should be clarified here. When this book refers to "Paul saying" or "Paul writing" something, keep in mind that Paul is not the source of the instruction. Paul, as an apostle of Jesus, was inspired to pass along everything God told him concerning these matters. So even though Paul was writing these words into a personal letter, the message comes from God.

JOURNEY INWARD

At this point in 1 Corinthians, Paul moved on to other topics. We'll stop for now and continue into new ground in the next session. But now let's do something that's not always easy to do. Let's talk about **sex.**

As you've seen, the biblical standards on sex are clear and specific. To help you clarify those principles in your own mind, imagine you're in speech class. Your teacher has simulated a talk show to give you experience on a panel. The "audience" (your classmates) can ask questions and your panel will answer them. The topic is, "Teenagers and Sex: What Are the Acceptable Limits?"

Your teacher knows you're a Christian, so she has asked you to represent the biblical perspective of the topic—whether you really agree with it or not. She has assigned other students to represent the publisher of a pornographic magazine, a member of Planned Parenthood, and a number of other special interest groups. You quickly discover that you are in a minority and that if you don't speak out for biblical values, no one else will. What follow are the questions you are asked during the course of the day. How will you respond?

(1) "Who cares what the Bible says anymore? The Bible is old-fashioned, out-of-date, and unable to address 'today's' sexual concerns—such as incest, homosexuality, prostitution, and others."

(2) "Regardless of the issues, don't you think any advice the Bible provides is a little outdated? The New Testament was written, what? About 2,000 years ago? Do you really believe it to be relevant today?"

(3) "What's the big deal if two people consent to be sexually active? I mean, it's my body and I can do whatever I want to with it, can't I? Who are *you* to tell me what to do?"

(4) "Come on, tell me the truth. Don't you think somebody who isn't out for a little casual sex is a little . . . strange? Are you saying there's no such thing as a sex drive?"

(5) "What about people who never get married? Are you telling me they should never be able to have sex?"

Finally, your teacher gives each person an opportunity to summarize his or her position without rebuttal from anyone. What would you say during your time?

Perhaps from answering your questions you've come to the conclusion that it's easy to "know" what you think about sex, and even to "believe" it. But when it comes down to trying to represent your Christian principles in the face of criticism or hostility, sometimes it's tough to make sense as you present your views to others. (Remember that much of what we believe as Christians is "foolishness" to the rest of the world [1 Corinthians 1:18].)

You can be sure that God will reward purity of conduct, especially in the turbulent, emotional area of sexual temptation. For one thing, you'll never have to worry about immediate problems: pregnancy, sexual diseases, and so forth. Nor will you have complications if you do finally find the right person for you and decide to get married. But beyond those obvious reasons, you'll have the satisfaction of knowing that God is being honored by your body, and that anyone looking at you has a much greater chance of seeing God in your life.

So the next time you're encouraged to get involved in something that's sexually suggestive, remember that Paul "suggests" that you keep yourself removed from such activities. When you do, you'll discover a satisfaction that can't be topped by any other sensation—sexual or otherwise.

KEY VERSES

"Do you not know that your body is a temple of the Holy Spirit, who is in you, whom you have received from God? You are not your own; you were bought at a price. Therefore honor God with your body" (1 Corinthians 6:19-20).

FOR BETTER OR FOR WORSHIP

(1 Corinthians 8—12)

Good morning, and welcome to the First Church of Total Honesty. If this is your first time with us, we'd like to explain that in this church our worship service reflects the way things really are—not the way they should be. So let's begin as we stand and sing our doxology:

Praise God from whom all blessings flow;
Praise Him for the next hour or so;
Praise Him right now while it is chic;
Then we'll forget God 'til next week. Amen.

Good singing! Please be seated. At this point we'd like to greet our visitors. Don't feel too bad if no one here speaks to you for a few weeks.

I'm sure if you come for about seven or eight Sundays in a row, someone might eventually notice you. It's kind of hard to break into the cliques at our church, but you can do it if you keep trying. Why, someone just did it, let's see, I think it was the winter of '81.

It's time now for announcements. There will be no Sunday evening worship service tonight because everyone would rather stay home and watch TV. There's no Wednesday night prayer service either, for the same reason. However, all the youth group activities will take place as scheduled—the high school Bible study will take place five minutes before the Monday night pool party, the junior high group will have devotions on the way to their Saturday morning fishing trip, and the outreach group will meet at Jillian's house for tacos, game night, and, oh yes, to discuss missions opportunities.

Now let's take up our offering. Some churches talk about faith, cheerful giving, and "returning to God a portion of what He has given to us." But let me be straight with you. Here at the First Church of Total Honesty, our furnace is about to give out and our senior pastor hasn't had a raise in a couple of years. So if you people don't start prying loose some of that cash that's so tightly wedged in your wallets and checkbooks, you're going to force a Search Committee to sit in the cold and look for a new pastor.

Moving on, in your bulletin you can see that this is where Sister Eloise Kuputkin was to have some special music to express her feelings about her relationship with the Lord. But she is ill, and her medley of "I Gotta Be Me" and "My Way" will have to wait until next week. So we'll move right into the prayer. All of you bow your heads and take a little five-minute nap while I stand up here and ask God for everything I think we need. After the prayer, we will hear Part 16 of Pastor Smith's sermon series, "Worship Shortcuts."

It's not hard to poke fun at other churches who seem to be off track in their worship habits. But be honest. Do you always go to church because you want to pour your heart and soul into worship? Probably not. Many people go because their parents force them. Others like to catch up on what their friends were doing over the weekend. Some go out of guilt or habit. And if it seems really ludicrous to examine a church service where total honesty is the rule, think how much more ludicrous it must seem to God to see all His people faithfully attend church once a week only to "go through the motions" of worship.

JOURNEY ONWARD

As we move on through the Book of 1 Corinthians, it should come as no surprise that since the church at Corinth had problems of a sexual nature, they might also need some advice concerning their worship habits. Remember that Paul wrote 1 Corinthians in response to a letter the people in Corinth had already sent him (7:1). So when he finished answering one question they had asked him, he moved right on to the next one. Judging from 1 Corinthians 8:1, what was the next topic the people wanted to know about?

Remember that Corinth was a major city in Greece. The city contained at least 12 temples dedicated to Greek gods and goddesses. And the "worship" that took place at these temples included such perverse practices as "religious" prostitution. (As many as 1,000 "sacred" prostitutes once "served" in the temple of Aphrodite in Corinth.) Animal sacrifices were also made in these temples, and leftover meat could be eaten at parties or sold in the marketplace. The issue within the Christian church was whether or not it was permissible to eat meat that had been offered to the Greek gods and goddesses. Perhaps some of the church people had been speaking with the "voice of authority" concerning this topic. What did Paul remind them about knowledge? (8:1-3)

What opinion did Paul have of the idols to which meat was being sacrificed? (8:4-6)

Most Christians would probably agree with Paul. So what was the big problem in Corinth? (8:7)

What did Paul say was the connection between a person's diet and his or her spirituality? (8:8)

But Paul immediately qualified his previous statements. He had basically given everyone permission to dig in if they could get a good buy on "offered" Greek beef. But then he explained that there was one string attached. What was it? (8:9-13)

Paul occasionally ran into people who would question his right to impose standards on them. So at this point he gave a defense of his apostleship. What do you think Paul meant when he wrote, "Have I not seen Jesus our Lord?" (9:1—You may want to review Acts 9:1-6.)

Paul confronted his accusers with some basic rights that he was entitled to. What things did he list? (1 Corinthians 9:3-6)

But the things that Paul listed all cost money. So Paul then gave a number of illustrations to show why he should have the right to be supported by the church as he traveled and preached. What examples did he use? (9:7-11)

How strongly did Paul cling to his right to get paid as an apostle? Explain (9:12-18).

What was Paul's method of making the Gospel attractive to others? (9:19-23)

In what ways did Paul compare his spiritual discipline with the physical discipline of an athlete in training? List as many ways as you can find (9:24-27).

Suddenly, Paul shifted his teaching from physical education to history. But his point was the same. In 1 Corinthians 10:1-10, Paul went back into the history of the Israelites and compared their past with the present situation in the Corinthian church. The Israelites followed God (in the form of a cloud) and passed through the Red Sea. The Corinthian Christians followed God (through their belief in Jesus) and were baptized. The Israelites ate manna and drank water from a rock—miraculous provisions from God. The Corinthians observed the Lord's Supper, reminding them of Christ—the bread of life and water of life. The Israelites slipped in their faith and became idolaters, sexually immoral, testers of God, and grumblers. They were reprimanded by God in each case. And the Corinthians? Well, Paul's comparison was obvious. What was Paul's challenge to the Corinthian church? (10:11-12)

What tremendous promise did Paul give the Corinthians as well? (10:13)

HOLY COW

Paul then worked his way back around to the issue of eating meat offered to idols. He made it clear that Christians are to flee from idolatry (10:14). Any Corinthian church members who had converted from following the Greek gods and goddesses might be particularly susceptible to falling back into their old habits if "dedicated" meat was put in front of them. And he reemphasized that even though the Corinthians seemed to think that "everything is permissible" for a Christian, everything was certainly not beneficial or constructive (10:14-23).

So what rule of thumb did Paul leave with them for when to eat and when not to eat meat offered to idols? (10:24-30)

What was the underlying guideline on which Paul based his rule of thumb? (10:31—11:1)

At this point Paul turned his attention from the worship of foreign gods to the worship practices within the Corinthian church itself. It seems that a number of the Corinthian women were going to church without covering their heads. If you find yourself yawning instead of gasping at this horrible news, you should know that this matter was definitely a major issue during the first century. Women with shaved heads or short hair during this time weren't trying to make a fashion statement or start a trend. Women who removed their head coverings in public were usually broadcasting the fact that they were looking for a little action from any man who was interested. And a shaved head was a sign that the woman had been disgraced or was openly challenging the authority of her husband.

Even today, religious people debate the significance of this issue. Most believe that head coverings on women were only a cultural expectation of the first century and have nothing to do with today's religious practices. Others continue to follow the specific instructions provided by Paul in this passage. For what reasons were women expected to wear head coverings while men weren't? (11:2-16)

It might be instinctive for us to feel sorry for the women who couldn't even enjoy a worship service without some kind of headgear. In fact, you will discover in the next book that when Paul wrote the Galatians, he told them, "There is neither Jew nor Greek, slave nor free, male nor female, for you are all one in Christ Jesus" (Galatians 3:28). That would seem to indicate that women should be free to worship in much the same way as men. Yet it seems that the women in the Corinthian church may have been doing more than exhibiting their freedom in Christ. If their uncovered heads were a symbol of their unsubmitted hearts (to their husbands, or perhaps even to Jesus), then they were clearly in error.

More will be said about the intended relationship between the husband and wife when we get to Ephesians (in Book 7). But for now, be assured that when Paul said that "the head of the woman is man" (1 Corinthians 11:3), he was in no way giving men the right to feel superior in regard to their wives. The God-assigned goal of the husband is to develop the kind of relationship with his wife that God has with him (including compassion, forgiveness, unconditional love, and so forth).

Under such an arrangement, submission is something that will come willingly and naturally.

COMMUNION COMPLAINTS

Paul had previously praised the Corinthians for holding to the teachings that he had given them (11:2). But as he began another segment of his letter, he said that he could not praise them in the matter he was about to address. He said that, first of all, there were divisions in the church. And then he scolded them for the way they celebrated the Lord's Supper. What problems did he describe? (11:17-22)

What was the intended purpose of the Lord's Supper? (11:23-26)

What are the possible consequences of taking part in the Lord's Supper when you aren't really sincere about it? (11:27-32)

How did Paul suggest the Corinthians avoid the problem? (11:33-34)

Paul then began to explain that God wants His people to learn to work together. If everyone is rushing around looking for ways to fulfill his or her selfish needs (food, attention, or whatever), then the church as a whole is going to suffer. So Paul describes gifts that God has given the members of His church—spiritual gifts. And from the first, Paul makes it clear that even though there are different kinds of gifts, they all stem from the same source—God (12:1-6). Paul had mentioned spiritual gifts to the Roman church (Romans 12:6-8), but his list to the Corinthians is more complete. Read 1 Corinthians 12:7-11 to discover the gifts that Paul mentions. List them below next to the appropriate definition. (Definitions and biblical examples [in parentheses] are from the New Testament *Bible Knowledge Commentary,* Victor Books.)

(1)_____ Insight into truth about biblical doctrines (1 Corinthians 2:6).

(2)_____ The ability to apply doctrinal truth to life (1 Corinthians 12:1-3).

(3)_____ An unusual measure of trust in God beyond that exercised by most Christians (1 Corinthians 13:2).

(4)_____ The ability to restore health and also to hold off death itself temporarily (Acts 3:7; 19:12).

(5)_____ May refer to exorcising demons (Acts 19:12) or inducing physical disability (Acts 13:11).

(6)_____ The ability to declare a message of God for His people, just like in the Old Testament (1 Corinthians 14:3).

(7)_____ The gift to differentiate the Word of God proclaimed by a true prophet from that of a satanic deceiver (2 Corinthians 11:14-15; 1 John 4:1).

(8)_____ The ability to speak an unlearned, living language (Acts 2:11).

(9)_____ The ability to translate an unlearned, known language expressed in the assembly (1 Corinthians 14:27).

This isn't meant to be a comprehensive list of spiritual gifts, but it gives you a good idea of the kinds of abilities with which God had supplied His people. After He assigns spiritual gifts, it is important that the church members work together to make sure the gifts are used to their maximum. Again, as with the Romans, Paul used the image of a body to illustrate the proper use of spiritual gifts. Just as a human body has many parts with different functions, the church "body" is composed of many individuals with a variety of abilities. Using the human body as his model, in what ways did Paul illustrate the foolishness of people who ignore their own gifts and try to develop other people's gifts instead? List (or draw) all the examples you can find (12:14-25).

How can you tell when the "body" is functioning properly? (12:26)

Paul summarized this section by pointing out that, yes, the church needed apostles, prophets, and teachers. But it didn't need *everyone* to be an apostle, prophet, or teacher (12:27-31). It is essential that we all find our parts in the big picture and exercise our specific gifts. And Paul promised to show the Corinthians the "most excellent" way of life to pursue. But we won't get around to discovering what he was talking about until the next session.

It should be noted at this point that the issue of spiritual gifts is a complex and hotly debated one among many churches today. Perhaps as you went through Paul's list of gifts, you saw some that sounded unfamiliar to you. Some denominations believe that certain spiritual gifts (such as prophecy, speaking in tongues, interpretation of tongues, miraculous healing, and others) were given primarily to get the church established, and were only temporary. Therefore they are no longer given to church members. Other church denominations still practice the entire range of spiritual gifts as listed in the New Testament. And of course, some denominations fall in between these two positions.

You should check with your pastor to see exactly where your church stands in this matter. But keep in mind that spiritual gifts were given to unite the church as a whole. Whenever they cause division among believers, God is not honored.

JOURNEY INWARD

As we consider spiritual gifts and the other information we've seen in this session, it's critical that we stop for a moment and think about **worship.**

When the church first got started, it was composed of a remarkable group of people. Many wonders and signs were done by the apostles. Church members sold possessions and gave to those in need. They met every day in the temple and in homes. God was praised and the people genuinely enjoyed one another's company.

But in a relatively short time, the church in Corinth had lost most of the "sparkle" that might attract people. Instead, it had turned into a place where the individual members did pretty much what *they* wanted to do, without regard to the feelings of others. One member was having sex with his father's wife, and the church as a whole was proud of his "freedom" to do so. Church members bickered with each other over which apostle was #1. The observation of the Lord's Supper had turned into a first-come, first-served fiasco. People were ignoring their own spiritual gifts and coveting those of other members.

It doesn't take long to slip spiritually. In fact, the personal spiritual lives of many Christians parallel the growing pains of the church. When we first become Christians, we often devote ourselves to Bible study, prayer, outreach to others, and other worthwhile activities that will help us grow closer to God. But after a while, our enthusiasm drops a bit. Or we encounter obstacles. Or we don't see the same rate of rapid growth, and we stop trying so hard. Or any number of things happen that cause us to come to a screeching halt in our spiritual development. One way to be sure that we continue to progress as Christians is to evaluate our spiritual commitment at regular intervals.

So take a couple of minutes now and analyze your worship habits. For each of the categories listed in the following chart, put the things you're doing right in the left column and the things that need improvement in the right column. You may want to consider both quality and quantity of each of these categories.

PERSONAL WORSHIP HABITS

What You're Doing Right   How You Can Improve

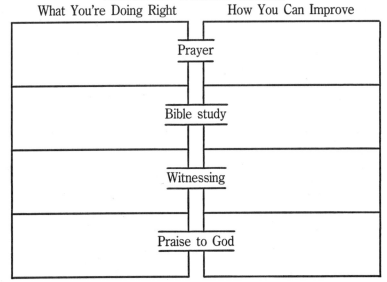

Prayer

Bible study

Witnessing

Praise to God

WORSHIP HABITS IN CHURCH

What You're Doing Right   How You Can Improve

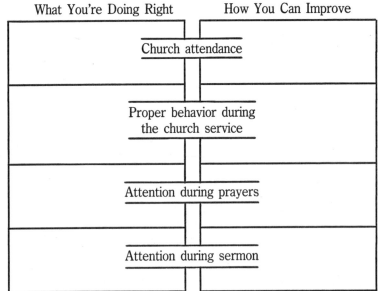

Church attendance

Proper behavior during
the church service

Attention during prayers

Attention during sermon

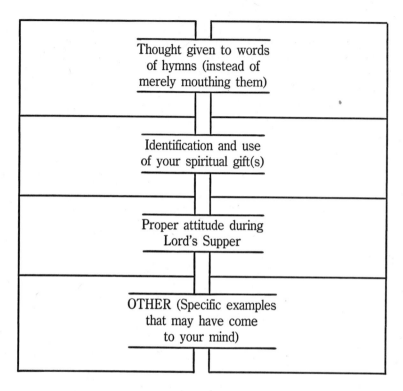

Thought given to words
of hymns (instead of
merely mouthing them)

Identification and use
of your spiritual gift(s)

Proper attitude during
Lord's Supper

OTHER (Specific examples
that may have come
to your mind)

If you've been honest with yourself, it should be clear which areas of your worship need the most attention. What may not be so clear is how important it is that you take action to improve your worship habits. It's not just a matter of your missing out on the tremendous things God has to offer. *Your* failure to contribute your spiritual gift(s) to the church causes many, many people to miss out on what God has for *them*. So start this week to plug into your church with a new enthusiasm. We're all waiting for you.

 **KEY VERSE**

"Now you are the body of Christ, and each one of you is a part of it" (1 Corinthians 12:27).

A MATTER OF LOVE AND DEATH

(1 Corinthians 13—16)

In February 1988, a strange story hit the papers. It seems that a family in Illinois had a sick father. The father was being taken care of by his wife and two children—a 17-year-old girl and a 14-year-old boy. Both of the children were honor students at their school, and they kept their classmates informed about their father's status.

Other relatives of this man were asked not to visit, due to his condition. But the family continued to practice their religion, which was described by the paper as "a religion that centers on preventive medicine, using dentistry, herbs, and natural healing techniques" (*Chicago Tribune*, February 2, 1988). And they continued to faithfully tend to the man, changing his clothes and bedding every day.

Eventually, however, some of the other relatives became suspicious after they hadn't seen this man for several years. A cousin initiated a police investigation, and a search was made of the house. But sure enough, the man was there.

The only problem was that the man was dead. In fact, he had been dead for a little while—eight years to be exact. And according to the sheriff, the family sincerely thought he was fine. They had continued to do everything they could for him, with no indication that anything was wrong.

Some other people involved were under suspicion. But the people who attended to this man had gone for eight years missing an obvious fact: When you're dead, you're dead. You can keep changing clothes and sheets. You can tell friends that Dad is only sick. You can keep mixing together those special herbs. But from a purely physical standpoint, most people who are dead don't get better—no matter what anyone does for them.

We shouldn't be too critical of this family. They acted out of ignorance, but most of us act out of fear. There aren't too many people around who are anxious to think about death. We don't even like to talk about dying. We speak in terms of "passing away," "going to be with the Lord," "buying the farm," or any other number of metaphors.

Sure, as Christians we know that we can expect to go to a better place. And we can look forward to an eternity of peace and joy in the presence of God Himself, who will wipe away every tear from our eyes. But it's that transition that's more than a little scary.

 JOURNEY ONWARD

We are going to work our way around to the topic of death, so keep your thoughts and questions in mind. But first let's examine some final things about spiritual gifts. Paul had promised to show the Corinthian church (and us, as well) a "more excellent" way of life. He had been writing about the various kinds of spiritual gifts and how we should learn to work together to use our gifts for the good of the church. But Paul wanted to make it clear that mere possession of spiritual gifts is not enough.

Remember that the Corinthian church hadn't done a very good job of using their own gifts for the good of others. They didn't want to use the gifts they had been given, and instead desired gifts they hadn't been given. And Paul had tried to illustrate how silly they were by picturing the human body as one massive eye, or one massive ear. Now he tried a different approach.

Paul asked his readers to consider someone with tremendous spiritual gifts—the ability to speak in tongues, the gift of prophecy, abundant knowledge, incredible faith, and an extraordinary willingness to give to the poor. He said that such a person might very well be worthless to the church unless his or her gifts were accompanied by one other special ingredient. What is the element that all spiritual gifts depend on? (1 Corinthians 13:1-3)

Why do you think this ingredient is so important to the success of our spiritual gifts?

Paul got very specific about the importance of this special ingredient. We should note that he never said that love itself was a spiritual gift. When we get to the Book of Galatians, we will find that love is a fruit of the Holy Spirit, available to all Christians and *expected* of us. So we aren't able to say, "Sorry. It seems that love just isn't my spiritual gift," as we walk all over other people.

Read 1 Corinthians 13:4-7 and describe the characteristics of love by filling out the following two columns:

WHAT LOVE IS	WHAT LOVE ISN'T

What is one of the major differences between love and our spiritual gifts? (13:8)

Paul wanted the Corinthians to see that spiritual gifts were given to help bring us closer to God. One day, when we're with God, we won't need those gifts anymore. But love is one characteristic that is needed now *and* in the future. What illustrations did Paul use to demonstrate his point? (13:9-12)

How does love rate on the scale of all the characteristics we're supposed to acquire as Christians? (13:13)

TONGUES

After establishing the importance of love in church relationships, Paul again turned his attention to correcting improper church behavior within the Corinthian church. Paul had previously established that all spiritual gifts were important. But now he is saying that some gifts should be given greater consideration in a church setting because they have significance to a larger group of people. For example, he cited speaking in tongues as opposed to prophecy. Which did he say was more important, and why? (14:1-5)

[NOTE: The issue of "speaking in tongues" is another area of debate. Some people contend that this gift was the same as that given to the disciples on the day of Pentecost (that is, that "tongues" refer to known, earthly languages—whether or not someone was present who could interpret those languages.) Others understand the gift of "tongues" to be a kind of heavenly language given to some people. These recipients of this gift don't know what they are saying unless someone with the gift of interpretation is also present. But under either assumption, the speaker is the only one who benefits from the exercise of his or her gift unless an interpreter is also present. Again, you should consult your pastor for his views on this issue.]

Paul compared speaking in tongues to instrumental music. What is necessary in both cases? (14:6-9)

What should we desire as we seek our spiritual gifts? (14:10-17)

What was Paul's personal experience with speaking in tongues? (14:18)

How did his personal experience affect his teaching on the matter? (14:19)

How can speaking in tongues be more harmful than helpful? (14:20-25)

What general rules did Paul give pertaining to speaking in tongues? (14:26-28)

What general rules did Paul give pertaining to prophesying? (14:29-32)

What general rules did Paul give pertaining to women in the church service? (14:33-35)

Paul was in no way attempting to put a damper on the spiritual excitement that was being generated within the church. So what was his motive in giving all these instructions? (14:36-40)

What did Paul want to remind the Corinthians about? (15:1-2)

UP FROM THE GRAVE

The Gospel was not to be taken lightly. Jesus had died to provide the salvation and freedom that the Corinthians were taking for granted. So Paul reminded them of Jesus' death, burial, and resurrection. And to confirm the truth of the resurrection (perhaps there were doubters in Corinth), Paul listed several specific instances when Jesus had appeared to people after His burial. Many of these appearances were recorded in the Gospels, but Paul added some additional ones that aren't listed elsewhere. List all the post-resurrection appearances of Jesus named by Paul (15:3-8).

How did Paul feel about being an apostle? (15:9-11)

After writing about the resurrection of Jesus, Paul made a natural transition into writing about the resurrection of the rest of us. It seems that some of the Corinthians refused to accept the teaching that one day all people will be raised from the dead. So Paul listed several logical conclusions of what would have to be true if indeed there were no such thing as resurrection. Read 1 Corinthians 15:12-19 and list all of the consequences of living with no expectation of resurrection.

After pointing out the foolishness of trying to be a Christian without believing in the resurrection, Paul tried to explain some of the basics of
the truth of the resurrection. In the Old Testament, the people of God
had been instructed to pause as they began the first grain harvest of the
season. A sheaf of grain from the first cutting was taken to the priest.
He presented it to God as an offering so God would be praised for the
entire harvest. The sheaf selected from the initial cutting was known as
the "firstfruits" (Leviticus 23:9-14, 17, 20). Paul used this example to
demonstrate that Jesus was the "firstfruits" of the resurrection of the
dead. In what ways was Jesus the "firstfruits" for the rest of mankind?
(1 Corinthians 15:20-23)

And as the One who made resurrection possible for the rest of us, what
will be Jesus' privilege in the future? (15:24-26)

As we read about the relationship between God the Father and Jesus,
we should notice something. If perhaps we tend to resist some of the
things Paul taught about order in the church or submission of women to
the men, we should pay close attention to this section. We know that
Jesus was indeed God. Jesus, the Holy Spirit, and God the Father are
equally worthy of our praise and respect. No member of the Trinity is
any more or less holy than another. Yet even within the members of
the Godhead there is an order. Read 1 Corinthians 15:27-28. It was
God who originally put everything under Jesus' control. So as Jesus re-
turns those things to God, He also submits to His Father. His submission doesn't make Him less important than or inferior to God the Father. As maturing Christians, we all need to learn to willingly submit
ourselves to others without feeling that it will diminish our own value.

In summary of this section about resurrection of the dead, Paul said
that if we don't believe in resurrection, we may as well party and die

(15·29-32). But resurrection was indeed a fact that we need to prepare for. So what did Paul ask the Corinthians to do? (15:33-34)

BODY BUILDING

Naturally the Corinthians would have questions concerning the specifics about what Paul had been telling them about death and resurrection. And as Paul anticipated their questions, he provided us with one of the most comforting passages in the Bible. He began with a simple but significant observation. He compared a seed with the mature plant that it produces. When you want to grow an oak tree, you don't plant a dead oak tree. You plant an acorn. That acorn then "dies," but in doing so becomes an entire, massive tree. So what do you think Paul was trying to tell us about our own deaths? (15:35-41)

In what ways will our heavenly bodies be different than our earthly bodies? (15:42-44)

How is Jesus contrasted to Adam in regard to our bodies? (15:45-49)

Why is it so important that we can count on a spiritual body when we die? (15:50)

When the time comes, how long will it take us to acquire our spiritual bodies? (15:51-52)

Is everyone going to die? Explain (15:51).

How are we going to eventually overcome death? (15:53-55)

What makes us so afraid of death, and how can we overcome the "sting" that accompanies death? (15:56-57)

As we peer into our futures and see death waiting for us, what should we do? (15:58)

Paul had dealt with some weighty issues so far in this letter. As he began to bring his letter to a close, he needed to tend to some business. It seems that the Christians in Jerusalem needed money. Paul had also mentioned this to the Romans (Romans 15:26). Maybe it was because of the famine predicted in Acts 11:28, or perhaps their intense persecution was affecting their economy. At any rate, the churches in Europe and Asia were pitching in to help. How did Paul suggest that money be collected for this fund? (1 Corinthians 16:1-4)

Paul then expressed his intention to visit the Corinthians again (16:5-9), and he tried to arrange visits from Timothy and Apollos as well (16:10-12). What final challenge did Paul leave with the Corinthians in this letter? (16:13-14)

In closing, Paul had words of praise for the household of a man named Stephanas (for their willing service). He also sent greetings from the people who were with him. (You might remember Aquila and Priscilla [v. 19] from Acts 18:1-3.)

And in spite of Paul's occasional (and necessary) harshness with the fickle Corinthians, with what words did he close his letter? (1 Corinthians 16:23-24)

Paul had certainly been straightforward in confronting the Corinthians with a long list of problems in their church. But he by no means had given up on them. His emphasis was always on removing the problem(s) and moving ahead in faith.

The next book in the BibleLog series will begin with Paul's second letter to the Corinthians. You'll discover that the Corinthian church still had a number of problems, but Paul's tone in his next letter is very vulnerable and personal. Even if you don't continue the series, you should read through 2 Corinthians and get to know Paul a lot better.

 JOURNEY INWARD

But now, try to get to know *yourself* a little better. This session has been filled with key biblical truths and wonderful promises, and it's hard to know where to focus our thoughts. So instead of narrowing everything down to one topic, let's concentrate on two issues as we bring this book to a close. The two topics are related, as strange as it may seem, and we'll get to their connection eventually. For the next few minutes, try to think through what you've learned about **love and death**. Let's start with death.

Because of graphic television programming, an accelerating suicide rate, and a number of other factors, people today begin to think about death at a much younger age than they once did. Not too long ago, most people were in their 30s or 40s before they began to think seriously about their own mortality. But now it's not unusual for teenagers to struggle with very real fears concerning death and dying. What questions do you have in this area? Write them below. (If you're in a group study of this book, be prepared to discuss them. If not, please take your questions to a pastor or caring adult. Most questions have good answers if you think them through long enough.)

Is death something that scares you? Explain.

Remember that even Jesus was reluctant to face death (Luke 22:41-44). But because Jesus *did* experience death on behalf of humankind, we don't have to be excessively afraid of it. As Christians, we can be assured that a loving Father will see us through it when the time comes and that we will be welcomed into His presence. At that time, everything that ever scared us or kept us from being what God intended us to be will seem puny and insignificant.

But once you've come to grips with death on a personal level, a couple of other important questions come to mind: "What about my friends and family members who *aren't* Christians? How can I handle it when they eventually die?"

That's where Paul's section on love comes in. Review your list of things (from 1 Corinthians 13) that describe what love is and what love isn't. If you're like most people, you have quite a way to go before you can say you're living by that standard. But suppose you began today to develop all the positive characteristics of love while eliminating the qualities that keep love from coming through. Don't you think you would attract friends and family members like a magnet? Everyone wants to be around people who are patient, kind, slow to anger, forgiving, trusting, protective, and so forth. It is through our love that people are attracted to the truth of the Gospel. It is by reflecting the love of Christ that we show Him to others. And once they put their faith in Jesus, they have the same promise of victory over death that you do.

We must not take lightly the promise that "love never fails" (1 Corinthians 13:8). So think of at least three people who need to see Christian love in action. Put their names below, and beside each name list some ways that you can show love to that person this week.

You can start small, perhaps with a greeting card or some light conversation. But keep developing the relationship until each person can see what true love really is. And you can be sure that he or she will want to get closer to the Source. At first, love and death may not sound like topics that go together. But if you have doubts, recite John 3:16 and think again.

KEY VERSES

" 'Where, O death, is your victory? Where, O death, is your sting?' The sting of death is sin, and the power of sin is the law. But thanks be to God! He gives us the victory through our Lord Jesus Christ" (1 Corinthians 15:55-57).

GROWING PAINS: THE CHURCH HITS THE ROAD
BibleLog Book 6

Please help us by taking a few moments to give us your honest feedback on this book. Your opinion is appreciated!

WHAT DID YOU THINK?

Did you enjoy this book? Why or why not?

How has this book helped you . . .
- understand the Bible better?

- apply the Bible to your life?

Have you used other books in this series? If so, which ones?

Do you plan to continue this series?

In what setting did you use this elective? (circle one)

Sunday School   Youth group   Midweek Bible study   On your own

Other _____

About how long did it take to work through each session?

Did you complete the studies on your own before discussing them with a group? (circle one)

Always   Usually   Sometimes   Rarely   Never   Did them as a group

Other _____

What grade are you in?
(Optional)

Name _____

Address _____

Additional comments·

SonPower Youth Sources Editor
1825 College Avenue
Wheaton, Illinois 60187